Simply Redeemed
Ministries LLC.

Embracing Your
New Beginnings

written by

Dr. Gary L. Neal, Sr., CPC, MAOL, Th.D.

ISBN- 978-1-957904-06-1

Library of Congress Control Number 2022913345

Printed and bound in the United States of America

First Printing August 2022

Editing, book cover design, and interior formatting by:
Dean Diaries Publishing

To order additional copies of this book, contact the author:

Simply Redeemed Ministries
s.redeemed@yahoo.com
www.simply-redeemed.com

DEDICATION

In loving memory of my father, Willie James Neal, and younger brother, Edgar Angelo Neal, who both were inspirational in me embracing my new beginnings.

ACKNOWLEDGEMENTS

I thank my lovely and amazing wife Marilyn, my sons Gary II and Darius, and daughters-in-love Jalisa and Melinda for your sincere love, encouragement, and support, even when my behavior wasn't the greatest and I wasn't easy to love. I thank my mother, Drusie Neal, for her diligence and unwavering prayers, and all of our encouraging conversations.

FOREWORD

From the fall of man in the Garden of Eden to CoVid-19 today, mankind has consistently been forced to deal with new beginnings. As the saying goes, the only thing in life that's constant is change. Nothing stays the same. Some changes are good, others…not so much.

Change can often be quite the conundrum. It can leave us unemployed, divorced or grieving from the loss of a loved one. It can also lead us to promotion, find us happily married or even millionaires with the right business ventures (or lucky lottery numbers).

A new day is always dawning, seemingly just as we finally settled ourselves into life's current status. So, knowing that the waves of life are constantly ebbing and flowing, it would serve us well to embrace the reality of change and endeavor to ride waves of our new beginnings.

This is what Dr. Gary Neal (aka my big brother) focuses our attention on in this book. Having borne witness to much of his upbringing and throughout his life, I can personally attest to the fact that Dr. Neal is one who is well qualified to address the topic of change and new beginnings.

This book comes at a time when the world has undergone a global seismic shift in the way we live.

Solid directional focus has become paramount in these times of great uncertainty.

But no matter what new scenario change may bring us, embracing our new beginning is the only way to grow from where we are and to see a future we never knew could exist.

As you read this book, may the changes that you've endured and those that are yet to come bring you to a well-lit path that helps you to see a new life and a new you. May it help you to embrace your new beginnings.

- ***Pastor Douglas M. Neal***

I am so proud of my husband, Dr. Gary L. Neal, Sr. and all his accomplishments especially writing this book! Being married thirty plus years, I have witnessed most of the new beginnings that God has allowed him to experience. Gary has always been a person that has tried to help others excel not only in their personal lives, but in their relationship with God and this book says it all, Embracing Your New Beginnings. I pray that you not only enjoy reading this book as I did, but let it teach you to take advantage of every situation that life will bring and embracing it as a new beginning. That is the message that Gary was delivering when he wrote it.

- ***His loving wife, Marilyn Neal***

Table of Contents

INTRODUCTION

Respectfully, we must start with the Holy Bible when talking about new beginnings. The Holy Bible not only expresses the most important new beginning to us that God created the world; more significantly, it articulates who God is. It reveals God's personality, character, and design for his creation – His new beginning. It also discloses God's most sincere desire: to communicate and fellowship with the people he created.

God took the ultimate step concerning fellowship with us through his amazing visit to this world in the person of his Son, Jesus Christ. We can recognize and appreciate how God created the universe in a very personal way. The heavens and the earth are here. We are here. God created all that we see, understand, and experience. The book of Genesis begins, *"God created the heavens and the earth."* It is here where we begin the most exciting, fulfilling, and embraceable new beginning imaginable. However, even in our own imagination, new beginnings can be somewhat intimidating, and quite frankly, a bit scary. So why do you fear to embrace our new beginnings? We all know and accept that difficult times are simply and realistically a part of our life. James 1:3 reminds us that *"because you know that the testing of our faith produces perseverance."* In other words, our trials come to make us stronger and better.

Unfortunately, the struggle that come with our trials can be exhausting, frustrating, and we can't wait to start a new beginning. We should consider every day as the beginning of a new, better, and happier life, filled with God promises and blessings. Every day should begin with affirmations of joy, peace with expectancy in our hearts that great and amazing things are going to happen. *"Even the greatest was once a beginner. Don't be afraid to take that first step"* (Muhammad Ali). So embrace all of your new beginnings and enjoy the journey!

A Prayer for Embracing Our New Beginnings

Heavenly Father, thank You for the blessed opportunities to have and embrace our new beginnings. So many times, we've wandered away from our relationship with You. In our times of suffering and burden, we choose to manage things on our own. Periods of defeat, resentment, disappointments, and grief have consumed our minds and spirit. However, it's in those conflicting times, we choose to stay absent from You. We ignore seeking Your help. Father, please forgive us. You are the way, the truth, and the light. We pray once again for you to direct us along the pathway to a new beginning in life. Please shelter us with Your inclusive love, protection, and mercy. Please permit us to express Your love to others we encounter as we embark upon new journeys. Thank You, Father, for Your loving-kindness, compassion, and forgiveness. Thank You for searching and discovering us again, and again, and again. Thank You for never parting from us. You are truly the Alpha and Omega, the

2

beginning and the end. Thank You, Father, that just as I can trust You with my accomplishments, I can also trust You with my completions and what doesn't seem sensible to me. I have faith that You are in control and are guiding my future in accordance to Your will and purpose. In the matchless and precious name of our Lord and Savior Jesus Christ, Amen.

CHAPTER ONE

New Beginnings

New beginnings, fresh starts, and greater opportunities seem to be the headliners of all our prayers. However, in most cases, it seems as if the same old thing occurs – wake up, go to work, come home, and so forth. So how do you truly build upon a new beginning? How do you take advantage of a fresh start? And how do you recognize and capitalize on greater opportunities? I have learned that the best start is a strong start. Scripture says that we are new creations in Christ as "the old has passed away; behold, the new has come" (2 Corinthians 5:17). F. Scott Fitzgerald stated, *"It's never too late to become who you want to be. I hope you live a life that you're proud of, and if you find that you're not, I hope you have the strength to start over."*

Whether you're new to Christianity and Jesus Christ or starting a different kind of new chapter in your life, look to the Word of God for wisdom and confidence to live righteously with bravery. It doesn't matter when you decide to embark upon your new beginnings. Just be sure to take advantage of the opportunity. Life should be a memorable and exciting journey that contains unlimited possibilities. So be encouraged to embrace a new beginning with the strength of the Lord.

5

The Bible in Genesis 1:1 says that *"In the beginning God created..."* He created! Everything that precedes after this statement is from the mind and thoughts of God. God didn't need to create the heaven and earth. He chose to create it. God also created mankind (us) in his image (Genesis 1:27). Therefore, in the beginning of life, mankind became a reflection of God's glory; everything about us, our creativity, our ingenuity. For instance, Adam and Eve in Genesis 2, were the highlight of God's creation – the very reason why God made the world.

Unfortunately, they didn't always live the way that God had intended. Therefore, God started over. Does that mean that God failed or made a mistake? Absolutely not! It means, as an example to us, we learn that through our mistakes, we can discover very significant lessons about how God desires us to live. God started over because He knew that we needed an example on getting things right as human beings.

God knowingly and intentionally paved the way for His Son, Jesus Christ, who was born into the world as our Lord and Savior as the only sin-free human being. What appeared to be a mistake was merely God's perfect and divine design at work on our behalf. Our vision, our speech, and our determination are the image of God. So, not only can we see as God sees, but we also can speak things into existence. In the beginning, God spoke, and galaxies spun into place, stars marked the heavens, and planets began revolving around their suns – words of overwhelming, limitless, unleashed power. He spoke again, and the waters and lands were filled with plants and creatures, running, swimming, growing, and reproducing – words of stimulation, breathing pulsating life.

Again, he spoke, and man and woman were formed, thinking, speaking, and loving – words of personal and creative glory. Everlasting, immeasurable, unlimited – he was, is, and always will be the Maker and Lord of all that exists. We can create great things because we bear the image and likeness of God. Therefore, like God, we too, possess the ability to see our new beginnings from start to finish. Our lives are a series of new beginnings and finishes. Jesus Christ, who is the author and finisher of our faith (Hebrew 12:2), who, despite the hardship and shame He endured, completed his divine assignment. We can complete ours! Jesus Christ is our best example of finishing the work God the Father has set before us. The start of a new beginning is the most critical and exciting part of the journey. Like God, he has given us the ability to create something out of nothing. We can take our thoughts, ideas, vision, and words and start something great. The time that we are born until the time we expire is important. The dash between our starts and finishes also has great significance in our new beginnings.

New beginnings are sure to occur in every facet of your life. Whether starting a business, going to school, starting a family, starting and/or leading ministries, etc., how we journey makes the difference. So, journey well! One day, my newest daughter-in-love sent me a video of my youngest grandson brushing his teeth for the very first time. As common and simple a task as it is for an adult or an older child, I found myself excited for him, to be able to witness one of his many new beginnings. For my grandson and daughter-in-love, it was the beginning of something new in their lives. Their mother/son instinctive connection and communication were the key to their successful navigation through this time in each other lives.

It reminded me of God's love and care for us; how He gently weans us into our new beginnings and newness of life, as we mature both physically and spiritually. Communication and networking in any phase of life are extremely powerful and relational tools for beginning and developing new partnerships. I remember an old saying, "Closed mouths don't get fed." As true as that may be, it was also a reminder that closed mouths can't feed either. Contemporary Gospel artist, Trent Jones, sings a song, "Open Your Mouth and Say Something."

Proverbs 10:11(a) says that *"The mouth of the righteous is a fountain of life,..."* In other words, it's equally important to spew out words of edification, comfort, and counsel. Speak up! Your voice and words are a major part of the initiation, development and networking process. A lot depends on us stepping out of our comfort zones and embracing the initiation process. Yes, it can be scary, but this part of the process is necessary.

I'm also reminded in the book of Esther 4:14, Mordecai told his niece, Queen Esther, *"For if you remain silent at this time, relief and deliverance for the Jews will arise from another place, but you and your father's family will perish. And who knows but that you have come to your royal position for such a time as this?"* Esther, Queen to the Persian king, had a critical decision to make, to open her mouth and say something so that her people would be spared, or say nothing and watch her people perish. She knew that speaking out of line to the king could cost her life if the king was displeased with her comments. However, her uncle, Mordecai, reminded his niece, Esther, that she would have no part in the glory if she didn't submit to God's plan for her.

This example reminds us that we cannot allow fear to be the factor that causes us to lose sight of God's purpose for our lives. We must always accept that God has a plan for us in any situation we may encounter. We should know and expect challenges to confront us in our lives. Fear will always be a factor. However, by faith, we must walk with God, trusting that our moments of success will inevitably come.

In the Bible, Proverbs 18:21 reminds us that *"The tongue has the power of life and death, and those who love it will eat of its fruit.*" Since networking is such a powerful element of initiating and establishing new beginnings, the tongue (your mouth) has the potential to set up a successful and prosperous journey and partnership. However, the tongue (your mouth) can also speak evil. If used for evil purposes, undesired consequences will be the net results. New beginnings are to be embraced every day that God allows us to experience life. Why would we want to be captive and locked in a world of stagnation, mediocrity, and status quo? We serve a God of plenty, overflowing abundance, and more than enough! God has so much in store for us. Starting new beginnings challenges us to think outside the box and tenaciously pursue the vision and purpose God has set before us.

New beginnings are the developmental stages of formulating innovative and creative ideas critical to the process. The beginning has always been my favorite part of the development process. Plato, the Athenian philosopher, once stated, "The beginning is the most important part of the work." I firmly agree. Beginning's form everything that occurs after them. With meticulous preparation and a thoughtful approach, your beginning can establish all that comes after it.

Beginnings offers countless opportunities to reinvent yourself and explore parts of yourself you may have never known had it not been for the initial thinking process. New beginnings also challenge us to gradually move beyond the norm and exercise our God-given creative skills. As you embrace your new beginnings, your mind begins to create new illusions of all the possibilities that can be accomplished. Your mind no longer accepts the old, outdated, obsolete way of thinking. A mind led by the Holy Spirit can do great things and make amazing things happen that can and will be fruitful; fruit you can eat and enjoy!

O taste and see that the Lord is good! The Bible tells us in 2 Corinthians, *"Therefore, if anyone is in Christ, the new creation has come: The old has gone, the new is here!"* However, old habits, unhealthy thoughts, and doubting your abilities and creativity just don't disappear. We must practice and exercise good and creative thoughts. The words, "in Christ" are the key to the passage. In Christ, old things are passed away, and all things have become new. Unfortunately, "in us," not all this is true yet. However, as we faithfully journey and grow in our Christian life, the creative thoughts we practice will gradually correspond with our desired position. But what happens when you begin new journeys that constantly meet with failure? Well, if you're anything like me, you can sometimes find yourself in situations or moments that force you to question if you're on the right road. Sometimes we're only left with one choice after a failure: starting over. That's when you start questioning yourself: What should I do? How do I start over? What steps should I take? Though things may look bleak, don't give up and keep a positive attitude.

Don't ever be afraid to start over. The good thing about starting over is that you're not starting from scratch this time. You're starting from experience. Your experiences build confidence to assure you that things will soon work out in your favor.

CHAPTER TWO

Starting Over

Peatures. They have a tendency to plant seeds of doubt, discord, disappointments, and frustrations in your mind. If you allow this kind of negativity in your mind, it has the strong potential to keep you from living a full and productive life. The important thing is not to allow your failures and the people who remind you of them to stop you from moving forward. Each day produces new challenges, but they also offer new opportunities. You don't need a new day to start over. You only need a new mindset. Romans 8:5 reminds us that *"Those who live according to the flesh have their minds set on what the flesh desires; but those who live in accordance with the Spirit have their minds on what the Spirit desires."*

When we yield to Holy Spirit, we can rise above our flesh and think, speak, act, and live for those things that are eternal. Jesus offers us avenues of escape from all negativities. We can be assured that our failures are merely building blocks to our success. Romans 8:28 says that *"And we know that in all things God works for the good of those who love him, who have been called according to his purpose"*. So, stand strong through your failures. Ignore the naysayers. Never give up!

Unfortunately, sometimes we are the reasons for our failures because of our disobedience to God, moving outside of His Will, and losing focus of the vision and purpose. However, I have learned to draw positive energy from my failures. I no longer see my failures as simply failures. I see them as beautiful reflections of what I have been through, and I convert them into the positive energy that drives and pushes me stronger and more determined than I was prior to my failures and setbacks. Disobedience comes with a price… chastisement and punishment.

However, if we keep looking back on yesterday's failures and disappointments, we become our own enemy. You can't reach for anything new if your hands are still full of yesterday's failures. I recall in Exodus 16, when the Israelites were traveling through the wilderness on the road to the Promised Land, God blessed them with a fresh supply of manna (provisions) every morning. Although it was to only last for one day, some of them didn't adhere to Moses' (God's) instructions and tried to hold on to the old manna (provisions), and it decayed. When you hold on to old manna (provisions) – what God used to do, friends who were good for a period of time, a position that you're scared of walking away from – it decays. It will never nourish you. You'll never grow.

Perhaps you've relished a friendship for a while, but at some point, you realize you've matured beyond the relationship. Or maybe what used to challenge and motivate you about your job doesn't do it for you any longer. You sense God telling you to expand your thinking, to leave your comfort zone, but you're afraid. You're left wondering why you're not passionate and fervent, why you're not growing. It's because that manna (provision) is old; it's not nourishing you. God has new beginnings for you. He's a God of freshness and newness. The manna (provision) was only temporary. God has new provisions headed your way. So, let go of the decayed and old, and get ready for the fresh and new.

Author Emily Acker stated, *"As long as you're still alive, you always have the chance to start over."* God has a fail-proof plan for our lives, and He tells us in His Word in Jeremiah 29:11, *"For I know the thoughts that I have toward you, saith the Lord, thoughts of peace and not of evil, to give you an expected end."* For anyone that has ever doubted God and have gone through times of despair, contemplating whether God has our back, this Scripture should serve as a motivational reminder that God is adamant on playing the long game concerning your life. However, you, too, must be in it for the long haul if you're looking to successfully start over and experience your new beginning. New Beginnings from history's greatest leaders, everyone from Reverend Dr. Martin Luther King, Jr., Mahatma Ghandi, and numerous biblical iconic leaders, can help light your path to a fresh start. Whether you're building a new business or facing a major change in your life, beginnings can be intimidating. Starting over or starting something new often leads to feelings of fear and uncertainties. Taking a risk is usually not easy, but it's often part of new beginnings.

But you don't have to be afraid of beginnings. Starting something new brings new opportunities and it can be inspiring. You'll likely learn important lessons about yourself. In addition, your new beginning may just be the start of something sensational and life-changing. Our faith is knowing that God has great things in store for us. Faith is confiding in God, living with intention, in peace, joy, and in abundance. We must learn how to get past our past and live a devoted life with faith and purpose. Reverend Dr. Martin Luther King, Jr. once stated, *"Faith is taking the first step even when you don't see the whole staircase."* In other words, an element of what makes starting something new frightening is that it's *frequently* encircled by doubt. You may not know what the outcomes will be or have any indication of how you will get there, so executing that initial step takes courage, confidence, and even faith. Eventually, you need to trust in yourself, your strategy, and the journey you're about to take.

Nevertheless, more importantly, you will need to trust God and His process. Don't get me wrong, I'm a proponent of scrapping and not wasting any time with what doesn't work and starting over. However, the unfortunate thing about starting over again is that it can be hard because you must hit that reset button to go through what you've already gone through. It may also involve the probability of you having to confront similar difficulties you've already conquered. Numbers 20:1 reminds us that *"In the first month the whole Israelite community arrived at the Desert of Zin, and they stayed at Kadesh. There Miriam died and was buried."* I mention this because it's important to understand that God may allow great time, trial, and tribulations to be between you, your vision of success, and prosperity. This portion of Scripture had been 37 years since Israel's first spy mission into the promised land and 40 years since the exodus from Egypt.

The Bible is silent about those 37 years of aimless wandering. The generations of those who had lived in Egypt had almost died off, and the new generation would soon be ready to enter the land. Moses, Aaron, Joshua, and Caleb were among the few who remained from those who had left Egypt. Once again, they camped at Kadesh, the site of the first spy mission that had ended in disaster. Moses hoped and prayed that the people were ready for a fresh start. My question to you is, "What and who does God need to kill off in your life that you keep giving life to? Are you truly and sincerely ready for your fresh start? Are you ready and willing to make the sacrifices it takes to see your new beginnings to completion?

Are you willing to trust God with it all? Are you ready for your seasons of blessings?" Well, if you're ready, I mean really ready, then heed to God's Word of *"being prepared in season and out of season"* (2 Timothy 4:2). Let's be sensitive to the opportunities God gives us. When we think of new beginnings, we often think of things that will turn out well and greatly benefit us and possibly others. However, some beginnings don't turn out so well. I'm talking about the beginning of sinful and corrupt thoughts that lurk in the carnal-minded individual. Many times, the thought of these illicit beginnings may appear to start well; e.g., adulterous and fornicating relationships, dishonest business ventures, gang-banging, drug dealing, just to name of few. However, in the end, the outcomes of these relationships rarely experience a happy or fruitful ending. Many times, illicit beginnings of trying to satisfy evil and lustful desires and deception may seem to go well and may even attract others to be willing participants. Nevertheless, seeds of discord, treachery, sin, will only reap a harvest of catastrophe, tragedy, hatred, unforgiveness, and so on.

CHAPTER THREE

Sowing Seeds

God allows us to be blindsided by these things, because He knows that on Satan's best day, he would not, could not, and will not knock you out! Stand on the promises of God! Galatians 6:7-8 says, *"Do not be deceived: God is not mocked. A man reaps what he sows. Whoever sows to please his flesh, from the flesh will reap destruction; whoever sows to please the Spirit, from the Spirit will reap eternal life."* It would certainly be a great surprise if you planted an apple tree that produced oranges. An apple tree planted in an orange orchard will still produce an apple tree. We naturally reap what we sow; this is true in various areas of our lives. For instance, if you gossip about your friends, it is possible you could lose their friendship. Every action has reactionary results. The Bible tells us that if you plant to please your own desires, you will reap a crop of crap, sorrow, and evil.

However, if you plant to please God, you'll reap joy and everlasting life. So, the question is, "What kind of seeds are you sowing?" The truth of the matter is that reaping what we sow is great for those who sow good ways. Still, it's a terrifying thought for those who are participating in ungodly activities such as promiscuity, drug and alcohol abuse, negligence of family, or neglect of others to increase their own level of success. We can't sow weeds and expect to reap beneficial fruit. We

19

cannot sow defiance to God and expect to reap His blessing. What we sow, we reap. Let us not mislead ourselves: We *will* reap the harvest of our lives.

Unfortunately, early in my walk with Christ, as a man of God, an ordained Elder, Assistant Pastor, husband, father, and so on, many of my own life lessons came from reaping the anguish and turmoil of bad decisions and ungodly behavior. However, I am grateful to God that during many of those times, God planted me under the tutelage and mentorship of Bishop Dr. Michael J. Love, Sr. and First Lady Dr. Karen Love. They stirred and planted within me the Word of God in such a special way. My heart was so receptive to their teachings, their love, and compassion toward me and my family. What I received from them were the planted seeds that would later influence my life specially and divinely. God used them to plant in me; that I may one day blossom into what God had truly intended for my life. I thank God for them. I love them forever. Then later in my life, God sends my family and I to live in another state, where the first people we meet are our current Bishop/Pastor and First Lady. Our move had proven to be an assignment from God.

It was at this point where I realized that God had intentionally uprooted us from the smaller pot and re-planted us in a place suitable and sizeable for our spiritual growth and nourishment that would also cause us to become planters. God has a special way of moving you from broken beginnings to fertile fields of rich, prosperous, and successful soil; fields where not only do you reap the benefits of heaven, but you can now sow into others your testimony of being an overcomer. What a mighty God we serve! Looking back over my life, there were many beginnings I experienced. Some good, some bad. However, there were two beginnings I would deeply struggle with for many years: the death of my father and younger brother. I never considered the inevitable experience of death in my immediate family. In 1992, my father passed away unexpectedly from a massive heart attack. I was thirty years old when my father died. Just when we were able to connect and communicate with each other on a spiritual level, just like that, he was gone. My life changed dramatically. In my thoughts and feelings, I felt that this was a "new beginning" God could have kept to himself.

At the time, I was the eldest of three sons, a recently married father of two, and a young police officer. My father was also a Chicago Police Sergeant. At that time in my life, I really wanted and needed my father's advice and mentoring as a strong father and successful and respected police Sergeant. I knew then that God was allowing me to have a Psalm 121:1-2 experience as He began to lift my head toward Heaven's Way toward the One who made heaven and earth. This was a major new beginning for me. However, I embraced my new beginning and moved on with my life without my earthly father. Unfortunately, twenty-one years later, in 2013, death came knocking at our family's door again. My younger brother, also a Chicago Police Officer, committed suicide. This crushed my spirit.

After all the emotions and feelings I work through managing with my father's death, I found myself in the same position of starting over with an inexpressible hurt. Some new beginnings come at a price we're unwilling to pay or expect in our lives. Sometimes unexpected beginnings caused by tragedy and trials can be very difficult to accept. It's not what we would have asked for, nor the way we envisioned accomplishing our vision and goals. Nevertheless, God gives us His word through Scripture that assures us that He is with us always and that our setbacks are merely setups guaranteed to work out in our favor. James 1:2-3 reminds us *"My brethren, count it all joy when ye fall into divers temptations; knowing this, that the trying of your faith worketh patience,"* and that *"And we know that all things work together for good to them that love God, to them who are the called according to his purpose"* (Romans 8:28).

Embarking upon new beginnings on the heels of tragedy, trials, and failures, may not have been how we planned our journeys. Still, it offers us a unique and promising opportunity to see and do things God's way. Prior to the death of my father and brother, I would have never compared my life or experiences with a woman. However, like Naomi in the Book of Ruth, who lost her husband and two sons, I, too, found myself in a place that I had never imagined myself to be. Through these difficult times, I was able to experience God in a much different way. His provisions, protection, guidance, and love, open my eyes to see life in a much clearer fashion. Gradually, I was learning to exercise and defend my spiritual authority, and take advantage of ALL God has for me, and what He was doing in and through my life. Death in itself starts a new beginning to the believer…eternal life. Fortunately, to the believer, it will be the last earthly "new beginning" you will ever experience.

Like Naomi, God blessed me with abundant mercy and love during very difficult periods in my life. I knew that God had a plan for my life as He clearly promised in Jeremiah 29:11, *"For I know the thoughts that I think toward you, says the Lord, thoughts of peace and not of evil, to give you a future and a hope."* What an amazing blessing! The Word of God is complete with heavenly and divine instruction regarding our plans, new beginnings, Scriptures about starting anew, and experiencing successful endings. God knows that living beneath the curse of a troubled world is not easy for us.

However, He understands that we occasionally fall down, but long to start over. God will always provide us with encouragement and hope through His Word. Many times, we initiate new beginnings from a happy place. Things are going well, and the vision may seem clear and concise. However, some beginnings can be complicated for various reasons. Often, we concentrate on the anxiety of the unknown which challenges us because the fear itself is a spiritual barrier produced by us. We can oftentimes become comfortable in a place where we feel safe and secure. It's equally important to remember that pursuing new beginnings will involve your prepared retreat from that level of comfort and travel through uncharted terrain, which can every so often be a daunting proposition.

It's important to remember that adjustments and insecurity happen. Adjustments happen a lot in life, whether we bring it about or not. Life is always progressing and seldomly remains the same for any period. Things can happen that will influence our lives in ways we do not anticipate but acceptance of certain change will go a long way in the direction of helping you with your new beginnings. So, when your beginnings become difficult to adjust and your focus requires fine-tuning, remember that God has you covered.

CHAPTER FOUR

Fears

"For I know the thoughts that I think toward you, says the Lord, thoughts of peace and not of evil, to give you a future and a hope." (Jeremiah 29:11).

God desires to provide for us an amazing future. Not one full of discomfort and misery, but one full of love and peace. When life creates sickness, grief, fear, and hopelessness, we can be assured that God is with us. He has thoughts and strategies for a future for us and he will not give up on us. Despite the fact that we know that God is with us, and trust all the things He tells us, truth be told, the journey can still be a bit scary and intimidating sometimes. Fear is our natural reaction to something we recognize as intimidating or dangerous. However, recognizing fear can help eliminate some of the reactions related to it.

Accepting your fears gives you power over your fears rather than your fears and anxieties controlling you. The Bible says that *"Through the Lord's mercies we are not consumed, because His compassions fail not. They are new every morning; Great is Your faithfulness."* (Lamentations 3:22-23). When we've made poor decisions and critical mistakes, we can be confident that He does not want us to continue in our fears or mistakes. He wants us to start over. He wants us to come to Him in repentance so that He can saturate us with His love, strength, and forgiveness.

Understanding your fears and anxieties will help you recognize the barriers you struggle with, and you can begin working towards discovering your individual resolutions. It's not mentally or spiritually healthy for us to dwell on past sins. Forgiving yourself of your past sins is critically essential because it guides us toward fresh starts and new beginnings. In 1 Samuel 12:20-24, David didn't continue to dwell on his sin. He returned to God, and God forgave him, opening the way to his new beginning. When we return to God, accept his forgiveness, and change our ways, he gives us a fresh start and a thumbs up on our new beginnings. However, it's important that we admit our sins to God and continually turn to him.

Then, and only then, are we able to move ahead with our new beginnings and fresh approach to living a godly life. So, speak truth, and learn to encourage yourself when your fears and past creep up on you. Remember, the words of our mouth are very powerful. Fear tends to cause our words to be negative and discouraging. However, positive and encouraging words can support you in seeing new beginnings and possibilities in your life. It will begin to broaden your vision and thinking to many more possibilities.

Ask yourself, what fears are holding you back from what you know God has for you? How do you react

when fear arises? Have you forgiven yourself for your past sins? If not, why not? How will you do so?

CHAPTER FIVE

Seek God First

Positive passion, power, and encouraging words can have an advantage to your individual transformation and help you conquer your fears and anxieties. As children of God, adopted to sonship, we have the authority to declare and decree that *"No weapon that is formed against thee shall prosper; and every tongue that shall rise against thee in judgment thou shalt condemn..."* (Isaiah 54:17). Speak life, declare victory over your setbacks and watch God set you up for victory! Speak over your hang-ups and do just that... hang'em up!! See it, believe it, declare it, and watch its manifestation.

New beginnings are to be embraced. They are to be thoroughly explored and sought after as God has intended. Scripture reminds us that there is great benefit and fruitfulness in the seeking process. *"Ask, and it shall be given you; seek, and ye shall find; knock, and it shall be opened unto you"* (Matthew 7:7). Jesus is telling us to persist in our pursuit of God. However, there is a divine order for our pursuit. Jesus also reminds us, *"But seek ye first the kingdom of God and his righteousness; and all these things shall be added unto you"* (Matthew 6:33). All the opportunities and possibilities that lie within your new beginnings are unfathomable, and the learning potentials will be immeasurable if you will seek the

Lord first. This is expressly why it is critically important to stay focused on where God is leading you. Never allow people, social media, personal goals and objectives, and other desires to become more to you than your pursuit of God. Remember to always seek and give God first place in your life. I've never seen a cart pull a horse, so there's no need to try to start now. Seek God first. In examining my past failures, disappointments, and setbacks, they usually came from me trying to hold on to my old way of living. I continually breathed life in volatile areas and situations that left me with seemingly no way out. Many of my situations nearly cost me my life and my family. Lies and deception began to feel like the norm in my life. Have you ever held onto the past so firmly that you couldn't seem to embrace the present or the future?

I don't know about you, but my past seemed as though it had a death grip on me, and my existence and future were struggling to develop because of it. Then one day I remembered a portion of Scripture in Job 42:12 that moved me toward a revelation moment; *"Now the Lord blessed the latter days of Job more than his beginning."* It reminded me of how God allowed Job to be tested by Satan, causing him to lose his family, health, and wealth. When the horrendous trial was over, God restored to Job twice as much as he had before. Like Job, God began to show me something different, something new. He provided a place for me when I couldn't see anything but wilderness and desert, but I trusted that God was always there for me. One day,

God revealed to me through His Word *"Do not remember the former things, nor consider the things of old. Behold, I will do a new thing, Now it shall spring forth; Shall you not know it? I will even make a road in the wilderness and rivers in the desert"* (Isaiah 43:18 19). *"For behold, I create new heavens and a new earth; And the former shall not be remembered or come to mind."* (Isaiah 65:17).

Just like that, my spirit experienced a divine revelation and refreshing, and I embraced a spiritual refreshing that I had longed for many years. From that day forward, God first, everything else afterwards! Your new beginnings will always provide you with opportunities to experience personal understandings. Scripture tells us that *"Wisdom is the principal thing; therefore get wisdom: and with all thy getting get understanding"* (Proverbs 4:7). Evaluate all that you have come to know and be thankful for it. Everywhere you go and everything you do, view it as positive or negative; it is all learning that presents new opportunities for individual development.

I encourage you to consider your new beginnings constructively, face your anxieties and not allow your thinking to hold you hostage. God will provide us with a new beginning, and we will live through eternity with God encircled by His marvelous light. It is no secret that the most familiar fresh start is January 1, the beginning of every New Year. This is the time when many people make their New Year's resolutions of various commitments that usually meet with failure.

However, in most instances, starting over and getting a fresh start after any level of failure can prove to be beneficial. New beginnings bring about change. Change brings about challenges. Challenges brings forth results. Results produces rewards. Rewards creates your next step. New beginnings can encourage people to improve and succeed in accomplishing their goals and aspirations. In an article entitled, *"The Unexpected Science of Fresh Starts and Failures"* written by Nick Hobson, Ph.D., Leandra McIntosh, and Maryam Marashi (2018), they cited a recent study that looked at the effects of "fresh starts" on performance. They noted that the "fresh start effect," as it's come to be known, is the idea that a person can disassociate their past performance outcomes from current ones. Temporal landmarks act as a kind of mental reset button to help get us back on track and get us focused on our most cherished goals."

Even though starting over may not feel like the best of experiences, owning and understanding your mistakes can also be very effective when you experience failure before the restart. Scripture reminds us in 1 Peter 5:10. *"And the God of all grace, who called you to his eternal glory in Christ, after you have suffered a little while, will himself restore you and make you strong, firm and steadfast."* The writer Peter gives us a broader perspective on dealing with our sufferings and setbacks. It's also through this wider perspective that Proverbs 3:5 gives us the main ingredient in our faith walk to be able to bounce back and move forward, and that is to *"Trust in the Lord with all thine heart; and lean not to thine own understanding."* When we participate in manifestation, we find ourselves putting more faith in our own beliefs instead of pursuing God's Will for our situation. "Changing your way of thinking" was the most important idea of Jesus' initial Sermon on the Mount (Matt. 4:17).

Jesus confronted the people to change their thinking. Despite how many times you read through the Bible, if your thinking and attitude don't change, you will merely enforce your preferences and labels on the words you read. Jesus began his ministry with the same word people heard from John the Baptist, "Repent." Therefore, the sooner you turn away from your self-centeredness and "self" control, the sooner God will be able to direct and regulate your life. Allowing the reigns of your life to rest in the hands of God is the best decision you could ever make regarding the direction of your life. With God in control of your life, you're able to run with endurance. Some say, "It's not how you start, but how you finish!" Well, I beg to differ.

How you start a new beginning is equally important as your finish. Endurance begins with a made-up mind, a right spirit, and a clean heart. When I was a teenager in high school, I remember playing varsity baseball. I was good, really good. So good that I thought I had what it took to play professional baseball. I realized that if this chapter of my life would ever come to pass, my journey needed to start right now. Therefore, I did what I needed to do to prepare for this journey. Granted, I wasn't a big guy, but I always put myself in the position to maximize my baseball gifts and talents amongst the best I competed against.

Unfortunately, I ran my race like a sprint instead of a marathon. I lost sight of the big picture and became fixed on my temporal efforts. I took advantage of my "start" and didn't appreciate nor understand the importance of my beginning. Like a sprinter, how you come out of the blocks is just as important, if not more, as finishing your race. My education took a back seat to play baseball, so my grades plummeted. My prayer life weakened, doubt began to set in, and my vision became blurred and distorted. The outlook of my long-desired "new beginning" to be a professional baseball player began to drift farther and farther away.

One day, I realized that God was preparing me for something greater. Although I loved playing the game of baseball, God clearly had a much different plan for my life. One that would lead toward my destiny, satisfy my thirst and hunger for Him. One that would allow me to exercise my God-given gifts and talents in a more diverse and productive way. A preacher! Are you kidding me?! A preacher?!

This was definitely a new beginning I never asked for, nor could see, and surely not ready for. However, since then, God has been guiding me ever since, and I am still traveling by faith. I guess it would have been nice to play a game for a living, but it demands more from you than you could ever give to it. So, I thank God that He covered and loved me so much that he provided me His grace, guidance, and direction at a time in my life when I was misguided and easily influenced by the world culture. Marion Woodman once stated, *"There comes a time in your life when you know that the life you have been living is over and you don't have a clue who you are becoming."* This is one of the truest statements in my life.

CHAPTER SIX

The Invitation

New beginnings can cause you to enter a place of nothingness, yet offer you unabated vision and power, and unlimited opportunities and possibilities. This is what makes new beginnings oftentimes difficult, yet necessary and rewarding. To make the changes you desire, you must be prepared to put behind you the reassurance of what you are used to and confront the new and unfamiliar. Indecisiveness can cause you to accept conditions that are not ideal. Have you ever experienced a relationship or career that was not satisfying or interesting enough, but you didn't want to leave for fear of what would happen if you left? Many of us get hooked in the trap of comfort zones. It's logical. Sometimes it seems simpler to deal with what we know rather than accept probabilities.

Unfortunately, the desire to care for ourselves, often comes at a steep personal cost. Isolation, feeling confined, dullness, and senselessness can all come from avoiding change. If we never experience change, then growth is not achievable. Like the caterpillar that changes into a butterfly, we also must be willing to assume sacrifice or even death, to bring new enthusiasm and commitment to our lives. Short of the efforts of the caterpillar, no butterflies would ever emerge. To transform, you must be ready to embrace your new beginning before its manifestation and work hard, or eternally remain a caterpillar. Joyce Meyers once stated, *"God works according to the law of gradual growth, so don't be discouraged if your progress seems slow."* A caterpillar doesn't transform overnight. However, it endures the rigorous and tedious process of its total transformation. The Bible tells us in Romans 12:2, *"Do not be conformed to the pattern of this world, but be transformed by the renewing of your mind."*

Like the caterpillar, we are truly transformed only when the Holy Spirit renews, reeducates, and redirects our minds. If your attitude or character doesn't change or your heart doesn't transform, you will always be the same. Some new beginnings are more like transitions. Take, for instance, marriage. Transitioning from being single to being married is a major transition. In most cases, a wedding is usually involved. However, when we consider starting a new life with someone in the presence of others, it's important to consider the guest you're going to invite to the wedding banquet. In Matthew 22, Jesus spoke of a parable about a wedding banquet which ultimately speaks to us spiritually on accepting the invitation to eternal life; an invitation that he offers to us repeatedly.

As believers, it's important to know that God wants us to join him at his banquet; to be able to celebrate our new beginning and spiritual journey of divine marital bliss as one with Him, which will last forever. Always remain open and ready for God's open invitation to eternal life. So, the question is, have you accepted His invitation, or are you constantly rejecting his invitations? The choice is yours. But choose wisely. The wrong choice could cost you more than you desire or can afford to lose. While completing my Doctorate in Cultural Theology and Christian Education, I learned that revelation exposes or unveils some form of reality or experience through communication with a divine entity or entities. In the Abrahamic religions, God reveals knowledge of himself, his will, and his divine wisdom to the world of human beings. Revelation also refers to the subsequent human understanding of God, prophecy, and other divine things.

God clearly makes himself known as Lord through divine revelation, which is provided to all people through creation and human nature and specific people through events, inspired human words recorded as Scripture, and Jesus Christ himself. In all these different ways, God reveals himself as Lord, which is comprised of his control, presence, and sovereignty over all things. There have been numerous occasions in my life where before God allowed me to experience the blessings and opportunities of a new beginning, God was not allowing me to bring along old and dirty baggage. Unfortunately, on all these occasions, I was the dirty baggage. The thoughts and destiny God had for my life, had no room for the mess I was carrying around with me for years. God opened the floodgates to my despicable lifestyle and revealed the dirt and sin that held me back from accomplishing anything to which God had called me. He revealed my disrespect and betrayal to my marriage and family. He caused me to face myself for who I was at that time, but He allowed me to see who He wanted me to be at the same time. It was then that I realized that I was revealed but not erased! I thank God for the revelation and for washing me of the filthy stench that was spoiling me spiritually, and for opening my eyes to the things that were so easily besetting me. When God gives you a fresh start, He'll even give you a new name! The Bible says in Isaiah 62:2, *"The nations will see your vindication, and all kings your glory; you will be called by a new name that the mouth of the Lord will bestow."* God will not keep silent, or rest satisfied until the blessings promised, and the destiny he has revealed to you has been satisfied. God wants to make sure that all your new beginnings get the fresh starts they deserve, are fruitful, and prosperous.

It is important to remember that God has created you to be a victor, not a victim, to get off on a good start for your new beginning. So, energize your day and efforts by celebrating the blessings to come and the very best of everything God has exclusively for you! As you intensify your faith walk and personal relationship with God, He will equip you to be all He has intended you to be, and He will keep you from being defeated. Luke 22:31-32 says, *"And the Lord said, Simon, Simon, behold, Satan hath desired to have you, that he may sift you as wheat: But I have prayed for thee, that thy faith fail not: and when thou art converted, strengthen thy brethren."*

So, as we begin new journeys, we must learn two very significant lessons. First, our disappointments do not have to be the essential characteristic of our walk with Jesus. Peter was fragile and he stumbled, but because of his heartfelt remorse and repentance, the Lord's help, and the power of the Holy Spirit, the Lord used and blessed him tremendously. We must never downgrade anyone, not even ourselves, to the garbage heap for disappointing the Lord at one time or another. God is gracious, compassionate, and will forgive our iniquities when we genuinely repent. Secondly, the Lord can use our failures to prepare us to serve better.

Satan wants to thwart our efforts right out of the gate! He wants to ensure that all of our new beginnings meet with an immediate and disastrous end every time. You will be rejected, but it's not because something is wrong with you; it's because something is right with you! However, like Peter, Jesus warns us that Satan turns his attention toward us and desires to frustrate and enables us in our minds and efforts. However, You're about to outgrow some spaces and places. Don't reject rejection. Accept it and move forward! Rejection is redirection! Get ready for your new influence and affluence! You're about to move past powerless to powerful!

Remember, Jesus says, *"But I have prayed for thee, that thy faith fail not…"* Jesus is letting us know that Satan is trying to come against us to distract, discourage, and throw us off course, but there is no need to worry, Jesus is praying and interceding for us. Surely, Jesus will prevent Satan from overpowering us. **Struggles are sure to come. There will be times that your faith is shaken and your motivation to act upon your vision and inspired desires** can become depleted over time. Do you need the right motivation for a new beginning? Things may not always work out as planned in life.

However, you may work toward aspiring goals only to see your visions crushed almost immediately before being successful. Extravagant plans might stall, and the devoted work can be reduced to nothing in the blink of an eye. This is simply a reminder that not every day is a good day. *"Courage does not always roar. Sometimes courage is the quiet voice at the end of the day saying, 'I'll try again tomorrow"* (Marry Anne Radmacher). Live for today, hope for tomorrow, and if you are blessed to experience tomorrow, appreciate it, and move on. In other words, if you are having a bad day, it is best to allow the day to close and start over on the following day.

Difficulties and complications in life should not frustrate you to the point of foregoing your goals and aspirations. Personally, I've found that failures and setbacks are merely steppingstones towards your success. Therefore, while it is not always conceivable to be successful in every undertaking, what matters most is that you always bounce back after your setback. If you lack the courage and strength to start a new day after having a bad day, stay in daily communion with God. *"God is our refuge and strength, a very present help in trouble* (Psalm 46:1). Just remember that the life in front of you is far greater than the life behind you. So, look to the hills from which cometh your help, stay focused and keep it moving! Whenever you set your mind on things above (Colossians 3:2), Satan always wants to add his slideshow of various temptations to distract, re-route and deter you from your vision.

However, God loves us far greater, and He protects and strengthens us to defend our authority over Satan. Where there is a way in, there is a way out. 1 Corinthians 10:13 reminds us, *"No temptation has overtaken you except what is common to mankind. And God is faithful; he will not let you be tempted beyond what you can bear. But when you are tempted, he will also provide a way out so that you can endure it."*

James 1:2-4 also reminds us to *"Count it all joy, my brothers, when you meet trials of various kinds, for you know that the testing of your faith produces steadfastness. And let steadfastness have its full effect, that you may be perfect and complete, lacking in nothing.* For every attack that the enemy has, God has equipped us to be able to launch a counterattack that clears the way and guarantees us victory. Isaiah 57:14 says, *"And it shall be said, "Build up, build up, prepare the way, remove every obstruction from my people's way."* God wants us to trust Him with all our new beginnings and have the confidence to soar far above our distractions and setbacks. Isaiah 40:31 tells us, *"But they that wait upon the Lord shall renew their strength; they shall mount up with wings as eagles; they shall run, and not be weary; and they shall walk, and not faint."*

He provides us with this encouragement because he knows that we, even as believers, tend to become impatient. We want to see the manifestation of our vision and new beginnings right away. We want to know when things are going to happen. God wants us to wait with expectancy in our hearts, knowing that God will do what He has purposed for and throughout our life. God has promised to strengthen you and equip you with everything you need to rise above your distractions and difficulties. Not all new beginnings start off good. However, through all the setbacks, having a mind in line with your vision should prove that God is yet moving on your behalf and still has purpose for your life. So, if your faith is shaken, and if you're yet struggling to believe, accept His provisions and care for you. Remember, *"And we know that in all things God works for the good of those who love him, who are called according to his purpose"* (Romans 8:28). You're closer to your destiny than you think. You've never been closer than right now to the things you're believing God for. So, thank God in advance for all the things He has done and is doing in your life.

CHAPTER SEVEN

Investing in You

Embracing any new beginning takes investing yourself. I remember sitting in my office penning this book, and I thought to myself, "What do I have to give that can benefit others? Why would anyone want to listen to what I have to say? The answers to these questions came to me the more I invested my time into God's Word and strengthening our relationship. My retirement account, my career; respectfully, those things are all good. However, I realized that there's no better way to invest my time, energy, and resources than to help someone come into the saving knowledge of Jesus Christ. So, I ask God to use and guide my thoughts and pen as I began to journal all He was inspiring me to write, so that others may be blessed.

During my writing sessions, I began to see the simplicities of how God's plan for enlarging His kingdom was worked through His vessels. I am one of them, one person telling another person about Jesus Christ. The more I thought about this, the more excited and determined I was about writing this book. I've made so many financial contributions to my retirement account in hopes of financially securing my family's future. This book is my spiritual contribution as a part of my Great Commission investment (Matthew 28:19-

20), telling someone about our Lord and Savior, our best new beginning.

Unfortunately, like financial investments, my spiritual investments sometimes met with delays and even setbacks. However, just like the golden rule in investing when the market gradually or drastically plummets, was not to panic and continue to pray for God's guidance and wisdom. In 2008 we experienced a recession that caused many investors to take significant financial losses; some were even forced into bankruptcy. Due to being a conservative and assertive investor, I, too, took a significant financial loss. My previous investment strategies taught me a valuable lesson, particularly about "leaning to my own understanding".

Fourteen years later, because of our faith in God and the new beginnings, which included a new investment strategy, we have soared far beyond recovery into being able to bless others, both financially and spiritually. Now that is an investment with benefits! This spiritual growth period greatly encouraged and inspired me. It reminded me a little bit about Joseph's experience in the book of Genesis 45. Although I did not face the physical challenges and bondage that Joseph experienced, Satan tried to set me back by invading many years of my life and suffering huge financial losses. Nevertheless, Satan attempts to harm me failed. God allowed me and my family to recover financially and then some!

Thankfully, God's plans are not determined by human actions. Satan turned out to be one of God's tools to fashion and develop me for greater. What I love about new beginnings is that they are sure to create an action continuum that can potentially propel you into your desired expectations. Change brings about challenges, challenges beget results, results spawn rewards, and rewards create your next. When a person is unchangeable, they are stubborn. An unchangeable person is hardheaded and cannot be persuaded to change their mind, no matter what. You can also say that a progression, like the progress of a terminal disease, is unchangeable because it cannot be stopped.

Many of us say we would like to change, be more affectionate, or be more open-minded. People who are dedicated to their spiritual walk convey this consistently. However, people do not realize that the ego is "unwilling to change," and we live in a world of the ego much of the time. Unwillingness seems to rule us. When you declare freedom from the bondage of your mind, when you can walk in your victories, when you truly believe that *"No weapon formed against you shall prosper"*, this is when you experience real breakthrough. Galatians 5:1 (MSG) reminds us, *"Christ has set us free to live a free life. So, take your stand! Never again let anyone put a harness of slavery on you"*.

We must be able to declare our freedom from doubt, overthinking, distractions, and disobedience. We must stand and fight through these issues until we experience the freedom and peace that God has promised us. We should have a preempted celebration in store for the expected and successful completion of our new beginnings. Stop waiting until the battle is won before you praise God for your victories. You should be planning and starting your new beginnings with victory in your mind and heart. Victory is the goal of the process. You already have it, so flaunt it! Bask in it! Declare it! Believe it! Receive it! It's yours, so stand strong! It is there that you should find yourself deeply grounded in purpose and mission far greater than yourself.

Those who can truly visualize their victory, those who trust the vision that God has dropped in their spirit, will experience and reap the expected outcomes. Vision is a very critical component of the "new beginning process. You must have it. If you can't see it, you can't be it. Plain and simple. As clear as the vision may appear to you; unfortunately, others may not see your vision so clearly. In fact, others may not even believe your vision will or can happen. This is why I strongly encourage you not to share your vision with those with no vision.

Trust me, they will hate on you because of it. Believing that your vision will come to pass is all you will need in keeping your vision moving toward a successful completion. Not only are we to have exceptional vision in keeping our eyes toward heavens-way, but we also need to listen in our spirit to what God is saying, as well. 2 Corinthians 4:18 says, *"For the things which are seen are temporary, but the things which are not seen are eternal."* Do not let your vision be contrary to what we are hearing. Be mindful of what you are looking for and whom you are listening to. Satan has a vast arsenal of distraction tactics. He knows how to use every one of them with extreme precision and accuracy.

It's important to remain focused, not be discouraged by the evil things you see, which are temporary and start being encouraged by what you hear. What God speaks to us is permanent. Listening in your spirit will allow you to hear the confirmations of God exposing you to new opportunities, new relationships, and favor is sure to be in your future. The main concern you may experience will be regretting the wasted time for your entire life. Remember, that time waits on no one. Time is one commodity that you cannot recover. Once it's gone, it's gone. Therefore, it is imperative that you attribute value to your time. How you use your time has an enormous influence on your ability to prosper.

Accumulative efficiency and managing your time intelligently mean you will have more time to do things that matter to you, like keeping fit, traveling abroad, spending time with family and friends, having a hobby, or pursuing other ventures. I recall one day when I was driving to work, I heard the radio host quote a statement that made me think deeply about the adverse effects of procrastinating. She said, *"Wasted time is murder on success."* So, I thought to myself, *"Am I a time murderer?" "Am I wasting time doing nothing?"* Are you a time murderer? Are you killing someone else's time, hopes and dreams? If you are, then I strongly suggest that you initiate TRR (Time Recovery Resuscitation), commonly known as CPR (Cardiopulmonary

Resuscitation), on your time and breathe new life into your wasted time, and live.

Time management is critical to every new beginning. So, set yourself up for success and eliminate the process of wasting time in your life. You may find you have more time than you realize. Time is far too precious to waste, so get moving and keep it moving. Learn to pull yourself away from social media, which in my opinion is the biggest distraction and time waster of them all, especially when you are trying to focus. Minimize your socializing.

Socializing is cool, but sometimes you can lose valuable time in thought talking a lot about nothing. If you are not careful and mindful of the company you are keeping, you may find yourself sharing your vision and time with others who may not have your best interest in mind. Remember, time is money. You aren't giving away your money, so stop giving away your time. Benjamin Franklin once said, *"Time is money...Waste it now. Pay for it later!"* Time and money must be respected and spent wisely, or no fruitfulness can become of it. You simply cannot recycle wasted time. The only value of wasted time is knowledge. However, the time you enjoy wasting is not wasted time.

Proverbs 5:11 tells us, *"At the end of your life you will groan, when your flesh and body are spent."* In other words, *"don't waste your life or time, so that at the end, you'll have nothing in your heart but regrets."* So, if you are going to waste time, enjoy it. *"A man who dares to waste one hour has not discovered the value of life"* (Charles Darwin). We often encounter the expanding disparity between where we are and where we want to be. Life, we discover, gets in the way. It turns out to be too easy in this energetic world to complicate means with ends, the hustle and bustle with significance, and pursuit with improvement. Embarking on new beginnings will require great leadership from beginning to completion… a leader of one.

Orchestrating new beginnings don't start out very well, and we become easily frustrated when we don't experience the immediate manifestation of our vision. Pursuing your vision requires courage, commitment, and sacrifice. You can't allow failures and setbacks along the way to cause you to become stagnate. It is time to stir up your leadership traits and start moving in the direction of success! We have been empowered to speak what we want into existence if we'll only trust and believe. Joshua 1:7 says, *"Be strong and very courageous. Be careful to obey all the laws of my servant Moses gave you; do not turn from it to the right or to the left, that you may be successful wherever you go."*

I've always been impressed with the life and story of Moses. As a matter of fact, The Ten Commandments is one of my all-time favorite movies. Every Easter, I never miss watching it. True leadership is first knowing who you are. His self-respect and self-awareness sent a resounding message to me – if you don't respect yourself enough to be true and honest with yourself, you're no good to anyone else. Moses gave up fame, riches, prestige, power, and the throne of Egypt in exchange for knowing who he was genuinely.

This "leader of one" mentality is what so many so-called leaders lack and why they fail to be successful. Embracing who you are can make the difference between success and failure. Who are you? You decide. Joshua, the protégé of Moses, also impressed me with his longevity of loyalty to Moses' leadership for 40 years. Although Moses was an extremely tough act to follow, Joshua boldly stepped into leadership to guide the people after Moses' death to launch them into their new beginning. Nehemiah possessed great vision and perseverance during his new beginning and was able to carry out his task without being stopped by ridicule, fear, and false accusations made against him.

Nehemiah demonstrated his dependence upon God as he encouraged the people to complete the work of rebuilding the broken-down walls of his beloved city, Jerusalem. When your courage begins to weaken, that is a good time to examine yourself to determine why you're not growing and getting the results you've envisioned. Two reasons we become weakened are sin and unhealthy lifestyles. God will not bless your mess! God knows your heart and He sees all. You are not going to fool Him, so stop trying. Stop living the "treadmill life," running, but going nowhere fast, and let God guide your steps. Pay attention to what God says to you and what He's doing in and through you. Ignoring God will cause you to struggle, and it will stunt your spiritual growth.

Another reason we are weakened and fall short of experiencing the manifestation of our vision is unbelief. In Luke 1:19, God sent the angel Gabriel to Zechariah, who was sent to deliver his good news. However, because of Zechariah's unbelief, Zechariah was silenced and unable to speak until the manifestation of the prophecy. Zechariah's problem was that he doubted the One he supposedly believed and trusted in. However, because of his weak faith, the angel Gabriel's mission was altered from delivering good news to bad news.

Like many of us today, we have so many goals and aspirations that we petition God for. Still, we don't truly believe that what we see or the Scripture we read will ever come to pass in our hearts. Like Zechariah, we want to share the vision, but because we allow our vision to become clouded and tainted with disbelief and doubt, we lose the ability to speak about what we cannot see. Luke 1:22 stated that when Zechariah was amongst the people, he could not speak about the vision despite making signs to them. They realized then that he had experienced a divine presence that would clearly change his life forever.

The Bible speaks about doubters. Many of the people God used to achieve great things started out as real doubters. However, with all of them, God demonstrated great patience. Sincere doubt is not a bad starting place if you do not remain there. How great a part does doubt have in your readiness to have faith in God?

Let's take a brief look at others in the Bible that have had doubtful moments:

(1) Abraham – When told he would be a father in old age

(2) Sarah – When she heard she would be a mother in old age

(3) Moses – When told to return to Egypt to lead the people out of bondage

(4) Israelites – Whenever they faced difficulties in the wilderness

(5) Gideon – When told he would be a judge and leader

(6) Thomas – When told Jesus had risen from the dead

Never doubt the Word of God. He has kept every one of His promises, and He will never let you down. So whenever doubt, the feeling of being crushed under pressure, or you are seemingly in a place of darkness, remember that grapes must be crushed to make wine, diamonds form under pressure, olives are pressed to release oil, and seeds grow in the cool of darkness. God always has the believer in a powerful place of transformation. Trust the process! Your new beginnings are just as important to God as they are to you. So don't panic when your mind gets clouded or reflects on unfavorable thoughts. Your mind is still working.

CHAPTER EIGHT

Step Into Prayer

Ensuring that new beginnings come into fruition takes sacrifice, commitment, diligence, and many times heartaches and failures. Remember that if God allowed you to see it, you can accomplish it. I heard a dear friend of mine and Prophetess say to me through social media, *"Prayer is always in order. A person of prayer prays. Periodt".* Prayer is the key component of all your new beginnings. Prayers for new beginnings in life can prompt us of the love, compassion, understanding and forgiveness of God. Whether we have stumbled to our knees in anxiety, tears in our eyes, and are pleading His forgiveness and one more chance to make the correct choices or we are praying for direction in life, God hears every prayer. We can go to Him in prayer at any time. Sharing our wholehearted prayers is one approach to get closer to God. His mercies are brand new every day.

In Scripture, God shares how His love never fails. Luke 15:4 says, *"What man of you, having a hundred sheep, if he loses one of them, doth not leave the ninety and nine in the wilderness, and go after that which is lost, until he find it?"* When we wander off and seemingly lose our way, He will search for us. How reassuring it is to know that we are never left alone. He is with us always. God provides us with the capability to have new beginnings in each moment. Hope and courage are found in Him. You will find security and comfort in your prayers for the new beginnings God has set for you in your life.

Scripture reminds us that new beginnings are conceivable, with God's assistance. 2 Corinthians 5:17 says *"Therefore if any man be in Christ, he is a new creature: old things are passed away; behold, all things are become new"*. Therefore, when we submit our lives to Christ, the old man has disappeared, and a new creation is designed. A new pathway is available for us. Zephaniah 3:17 says, *"The Lord thy God in the midst of thee is mighty; he will save, he will rejoice over thee with joy; he will rest in his love, he will joy over thee with singing."* This assures us that we do not have to be dependent on our mortal capacity. Trust and hope are found in Him. We are sure to experience failures and setbacks, and we will not always make the best decisions, yet with God, a new life will begin. Every time we stumble and fall, there is always hope and comfort in going to God and praying for a new beginning.

It is vital to the success of Christ-followers that we share in conversation with God through our heartfelt prayers, which can bring about comfort, relief, and peace. Going to God in prayer can fill us with His courage, grace, and love when we face trials, doubts, and new beginnings. Trusting God conveys us to a stronger and deeper relationship with Him. Through our words and actions, others will see the love of Christ. Then, the distinctive, everlasting love of Christ will be shared throughout the world. A new beginning is awaiting us each day. Go to God and pray. Thank Him for the generous and plentiful blessings he provided, for the love He imparts upon us in each instant, and for the compassion and understanding He offers to us. Thank Him for new beginnings and the close relationship we can have with Him.

I love how God can bring you out of unstable and volatile situations and place your feet upon grounds of serenity and peace. My prayer is that God would allow me to experience and accomplish all He has for me. Over the course of my life, I have tried initiating business ideas and various other personal investments and new beginnings that never met the expected success level. Then I realized my prayer life was weak; thereby, causing the results of my ventures to be weak. Little prayer, little power. No prayer, no power. I have learned to give God glory in all things; good or bad, happy, or sad. God deserves our best praise and all the glory. God revealed to me that my failures also have a positive purpose in my life. All the time, God had been trying to show me the way to my successful new beginnings, but I couldn't embrace it because of my selfishness, vain repetitious prayers, and lack of focus.

I know that am anointed and dedicated to the services of God as He fulfills His special purposes for and through my life. However, I remember early on in my life, I tried playing the seesaw-effect with my anointing by straddling the fence (Trying to live worldly and spiritually). Are you allowing things into your life that are impeding your anointing? Let me advise you that you'll never benefit from an anointing that you disgrace publicly. Before an anointing will come into action, there must be a committed mindset. Therefore, purging is an essential component. Self-inventory is critical; ask God to take inventory of our thoughts, beliefs and objectives, and blood-wash us from the inside out. Nothing can or will ever replace a refreshing change from God in your life. Material things cannot substitute the blessings that truly satisfy us and creates the joy and happiness in our lives. Keep God primarily in your life. Remain receptive to the Holy Spirit instructing and controlling your life.

In an article written by Jentezen Franklin entitled, *"The Five Ingredients of an Anointing"*, Franklin stated that, *"You need an ongoing relationship through worship, prayer, and the Word. You cannot sustain an anointed life on a stale, forgotten relationship with God. You need a fresh anointing. If you want to walk in the anointing of God, to live in the fullness and power of His presence you must be meek, upright, and humble. You must ask God to search your heart and cleanse you; keep your life rid of impurities that will hinder the anointing. And you must seek the Holy Spirit, an active and daily filling of the Spirit of the Lord in your life"* (2021).

To walk and operate in your anointing means that you have come to terms with the fact that what you are doing is of God, so accept it and walk therein. You should know in your heart that God has chosen you for something great, unique and exceptional. Therefore, embrace, use, and cultivate the fact that God has chosen you to do just what you do. Remain humble and teachable as the Holy Spirit orders and guide your steps. *"But the anointing which ye have received of him abideth in you, and ye need not that any man teach you: but as the same anointing teacheth you of all things, and is truth, and is no lie—and even as it has taught you, ye shall abide in him"* (1 John 2:27, KJV). Let this be the basis of all of your new beginnings. The anointing that is on your life attracts attacks. However, don't look at it as trouble, look at it as confirmation. Stay focused and keep it moving!

My prayer for you:
I pray that there will be peace within you this day and forevermore. May you trust God that you are exactly where and what you are meant to be. May you never forget the infinite and immeasurable possibilities that are born of faith through Jesus Christ. Amen.

CHAPTER NINE

Check Your Surroundings

There are sure to come moments in your life where you will need a positive change. Sometimes, people just need to start a new life away from whatever suffering, despair, concerns, or monotony that frequently disrupts their life. Determining to modify your life can be challenging because most people dread that it is too late to do something new or start fresh. You can easily find different ways to start fresh, whether you want to gradually advance toward such changes, or you may want to plunge all in, it is up to you.

You must get over that troublesome voice that tells you that you cannot start fresh, and you will appreciate that you have a world of possibilities and opportunities waiting ahead of you. Speaking of making changes in your life, occasionally changing how you do things will make you feel like you have a different life. We are creatures of habit, which means we relax into common practices and sometimes we cannot get out of them easily. You can also choose to change your routine 180 degrees if you want a life that is completely different from the one you've led up until now. Trust me, boredom is the killer of new beginnings. If your new beginning doesn't excite you, it probably won't excite anyone else. So, start integrating one new daily activity you normally don't do or swap a routine with a new activity to progressively change your obsolete daily routine.

It is so important to discover yourself. Moreover, to imagine where you stand on things, discovering yourself also means being at peace with the person you are. Discovering yourself means becoming more conscious of the person you are and clearly understanding your beliefs, ideas, individuality, aspirations, and visions. *"Finding yourself is not really how it works. You are not a ten-dollar bill in last winter's coat pocket. You are also not lost. Your true self is right there, buried under cultural conditioning, other people opinions, and inaccurate conclusions you drew as a kid that became your beliefs about who you are. Finding yourself is returning to yourself. An unlearning, an excavation, a remembering of who you were before the world got its hands on you"* (Emily McDowell). Discovering and returning to yourself can be uncomfortable. Therefore, you will be enticed to pull back from it. However, Jesus observed this inclination in the Pharisees, and He said they vindicated themselves in the presence of men (Luke 16:15). Additionally, He said that people love darkness rather than light because their deeds are evil (John 3:19).

They would rather not come to the light because the light uncovers their sins. So, pay more attention to the things that you're prioritizing over your relationship with God and the important things in your life. I once read a very intriguing and thought-provoking analogy by a philosophy teacher who described life as a jar. *"He placed a jar on his desk and proceeded to fill it up with ping pong balls until no more could fit. He asked his students if they all agreed that the jar was full. They all agreed. He then poured jelly beans into the jar. The jelly beans filled the spaces in between the balls. He asked the students again if the jar was full. They all agreed. The teacher then poured sand into the jar. The sand filled in all of the empty spaces.*

He asked the students again if the jar was full. Again, they all agreed. Finally, the teacher poured a can of soda into the jar filling the empty space. Then the teacher said, "Students, I want you to realize this jar represents your life." The ping pong balls represent the important things; your health, family, friends and passions. They fulfill your life most. The jelly beans represent the other things in life like your career, home and responsibilities. The sand is everything else; the small "stuff".

If you put the sand in first, there's no room for anything else. The same goes for life. If you spend all of your time and energy on the small stuff, you will never have room for the important things. So use your time wisely and focus on the things that make you happy! The rest is just sand. Then a student shouted, "You never mentioned what the soda represents!" The teacher smiled and said, "The soda demonstrates that no matter how full your life is, there's always room to have a cool and refreshing drink with a friend."
- Unknown Philosophy Professor

After reading this, I thought earnestly about what and who's surrounding me. I pondered what and who I'm allowing in my inner circle, which means no earthly good. My inner-circle assessment didn't look too bad, but I realized that I have a tendency to share too much information with people. You never know what people are harboring on the inside concerning you; jealousy, hatred, animosity, fear, doubt, and the list can go on and on. Satan is conniving and deceptive. Unfortunately, many people cower under their own disbelief in their vision, lack of self-confidence and most importantly, their lack of faith in God. They've conformed to their negative surroundings and became a product of their negative and unproductive environment. Satan would just love for your new and promising beginnings to be your dreadful endings.

When you're in a fight, physically or spiritually, there's a "mob mindset" that confronts you. For instance, if someone breaks out and runs past you because of fear, he'll more than likely cause a substantial remorse because you and everybody else will be frightened due to the action of one person which tends to affect the attitude of everyone. Now everybody's running for fear of the unknown. Fortunately, the opposite works, also – the courage of one person can encourage and inspire everyone. There are two sides to it. Spiritually, God wants willing and brave soldiers in His army. To God, size is not important; it's the heart of a man that matters most to God.

Deuteronomy 20:8 says, *"Then the officers shall add, "Is anyone afraid or fainthearted? Let him go home so that his fellow soldiers will not become disheartened too".* God knows that some have tendencies to allow the cares of this life to cause them to cower under pressure. Others fail to trust

God wholeheartedly and focus on the spiritual warfare before us.

This behavior can be detrimental and distracting to those who are focused. It has the potential to cause them to cower as well. Thankfully, God can do more with less who are committed to Him than more who compromises His will.

When we launch out in our new beginnings, understand that we have to be responsible to complete the journey in its entirety in every situation. God never sends you into a situation or on a journey alone. He goes before you, stands beside you, and walks behind you. Whatever situation you have right now, be confident; God is with you. God promised He would always be with us! However, there are individual responsibilities for us, first, to be obedient to God, and second, to be faithful and loyal to Him completely. If we choose to wander away and do things on our own, then we will endure the weight of our sin, but it is not going to end there because our sin will affect everybody else unless remedial action is taken.

It's imperative to remember that before the people of Israel went out to battle, God told the leaders to isolate themselves from anyone who was fearful and faint-hearted. God knew that fear would spread and dishearten others, keeping them from attaining victory. The spirits and attitudes of the people around you are transferrable. You're eventually going to become like the people you're around. Proverbs 13:20 tells us,

"Walk with the wise and become wise, for a companion of fools suffers harm." Notice it happens in the positive and in the negative.

I remember watching the movie "Fallen", starring the incomparable acting legend, Denzel Washington. Denzel plays a detective (John Hobbes) who attempts to track the destructive and murderous activities of the evil spirit called "Azazel." Azazel is cursed to roam to and fro on the earth without form, and he can switch bodies by mere contact, making him difficult to track. This is expressly why the people of God must remain watchful and prayerful of our surrounding and who we're allowing in our inner circle and who wants to get close to you. Don't be so quick to befriend everyone. Azazel can also be modern-day social media.

Everybody isn't your friend (Facebook, etc.), so stop putting your vision and business out there for everyone to see. Rubbing up against the wrong people can cause you to be infected. Matthew 26:41 says, *"Watch and pray, that ye enter not into temptation: the spirit indeed is willing, but the flesh is weak."* You have to be very selective with whom you choose to spend your time. If they're negative and critical, if they compromise your vision and don't have integrity, they're feeding you all the wrong things. They're going to keep you from elevating to the next level. So remember, never tell anyone your plans. Show them your results instead. You don't have to broadcast your plans to them, but you need to spend less and less time with them.

If you don't distinguish yourself from the wrong people, you'll never meet the right ones. It's dangerous to have people around you who envy and hate you. They look at you as competition while you're looking at them as family and friends. You should surround yourself with people who encourage and inspire you, who challenge you, and cause you to grow. It helps even more when you're grounded in purpose and a mission that's greater than yourself. So, as believers, we must continue to bless God with our reasonable service because He uses the right people to challenge and inspire us to grow and be at our very best everyday. God helps us be honest with ourselves, bold, and confident in being selective with whomever we spend our time with. So be mindful of your surroundings and who's surrounding you. *"Stay far away from negative people – they have a problem for every solution"* (Albert Einstein).

God will always provide networking opportunities and bring the right people into your life. Networking is not simply the interchange of information with others — and it is surely not about pleading for help. Networking is an amazing opportunity to create and develop long-lasting, reciprocally favorable relationships with the people you encounter, whether you are waiting in line to order breakfast, partaking in an event, or simply attending a training seminar. You don't have to attend every networking occasion that comes your way to be a productive networker. If you didn't pay so much attention to your cell phone when you're out in public, you'll find that networking opportunities are plentiful and all around and about you daily. While you don't need to identify precisely what you anticipate getting out of each networking opportunity, it's imperative to move into each event with solid objectives.

For instance, you may participate in an event with the desire to connect with new people in your profession and discover new vision or enhance your previous vision to share with your co-workers. I recall a Facebook post by my friend, Pastor Dr. Dexter K. Ball made where he said, *"There's power in agreement. Having the right believers in your life is an important part to helping in fulfilling your purpose and destiny."* In the book entitled, *"Networking, it's Your Superpower!"* written by my dear friend, Kesha Kent, she stated that she wanted her readers to *"remove any negative impressions we may have relating to networking. Get rid of it, and say, "Networking is my superpower."* I agree that networking and positively connecting with others is a key ingredient to experiencing the manifestation and success of our new beginnings. The Bible also tells us, *"Death and life are in the power of the tongue: and they that love it shall eat the fruit thereof"* (Proverbs 18:21).

This reminds us that we have the power to change things negatively or positively just by speaking it. So, be mindful of the words that proceed from your mouth. Matthew 12:34(b) says, *"for out of the abundance of the heart the mouth speaketh."* God provides us with the means to speak and plant seeds into the fertile ground to produce a plentiful and successful harvest for others to partake of its wealth and goodness. Productivity starts within us. As believers, we must trust and believe that God is birthing a new thing through us. There will be times when we will have to push and press our way through the pain and difficulties of

68

birthing new life. However, what God has ordained cannot be stopped. What feels like the end is often times the beginning. Philippians 1:6 tells us, *"Being confident of this, that he who began a good work in you will carry it on to completion until the day of Jesus Christ."* So, with boldness and confidence, open your mouth and say something positive, encouraging, edifying, and inspiring to someone, and enjoy the benefits of the fruit thereof! The best is yet to come!

CHAPTER TEN

Keep a Clean House

I love the endless possibilities and opportunities that each new beginning offers and another chance for a fresh start, especially in marriage. In fact, each day is truly a new beginning – a fresh start and an opportunity for transformation, reconciliation, forgiveness, spiritual growth, and personal development. A chance to be a better you – a better us. However, the real question is – will you accept the challenge to change? Will you decide on what is relaxed, average, and ordinary? The wonderful thing about this is that you get to decide. I don't know what situation your marriage is presently in, but I'm telling you that "right now" is offering you a fresh start.

An opportunity to develop and improve your marriage like never before. A chance to transform the things you know needs transforming – to search deep within and truly dedicate to being better. It doesn't matter how bad things are right now. I know things can get better for you. Things can improve. You can adjust. Your spouse can adjust. Your marriage can be adjusted. Leave the past behind no matter how disheartened you may be about how things are going. Isaiah 43:18 tells us to *"Remember ye not the former things, neither consider the things of old."* God wants you to know that even your past miracles are nothing compared to what God is going to do for you in the future. So, keep your eyes looking forward to the future. Forget about all the disagreements, your failure to get along, the disappointments, the setbacks, the broken hopes and the nasty quarrels about money and expenses.

Stop with the cynical and abrasive comments and impolite attitude. Focus on being kind and considerate to each other. Intentionally looking to be a better spouse and person is almost certainly one of the best ways to reside in the present, while creating a better future. Change won't take place immediately. However, I encourage you to decide on a single, common goal for your marriage and see it to fruition. Then rejoice and enjoy the blessings of the Lord forever! Not every new beginning stems from within a happy place. One of the worst unhappy places I can think of is starting a relationship/marriage over after an affair. Infidelity is probably the most difficult and continuous beginning process known to man. So, the question is, "How do you start over with your spouse after an affair?" There are several suggestions I could offer, but first, I believe it is important to understand that the dissimilarities between men and women are the various forms of infidelity for each gender.

In an article submitted by the staff of *Good Clean Love* entitled, *"How to Start Over with Your Partner After an Affair"*, it was cited *"Cheating men are more likely than cheating women to have an affair with someone younger than their spouse. On the other hand, cheating women are more likely than cheating men to have an affair with someone better educated than their current spouse is. Additionally, marked sex differences exist in the age patterns of infidelity. Women are far more likely to commit infidelity in their 20s and early in their relationship, whereas men's affairs happen later in their relationship and predominantly after the age of 40"* (2019). Per recent statistics, apparently, couples are deciding to attempt to work at their relationships, despite unfaithfulness.

Furthermore, married couples are accepting that it is not always the ideal resolution to believe that you can exchange your partner for another one or that this new, found love will outlast the previous one or be better. Infidelity is severely devastating to the family unit. The unfaithful spouse normally has no idea of the damage he/she is causing himself/herself or their family until the affair has been revealed and addressed. This is never an easy matter to deal with. Infidelity is built on dishonesty and deception. There are typically emotions involved, even if the emotions are remorse and anxiety. The shame and regret over hurting your partner or family are very real and agonizing. The pain of betrayal and brokenness constantly lingers and appears endless and unrepairable at times.

The victimized spouse may even have family or friends that would empathize with them to the point of suggesting separation or even divorce. But, God! Although there are various Scriptures in the Bible that address grounds for divorce, God wants to see married couples happy, full of joy, and moving forward together thriving in love. Thank God for His precious Holy Spirit of forgiveness and the power of redemption and restoration. New beginnings, which are spawned from forgiveness, has the power to produce everlasting results that can shift the impossible to possible, and transform the atmosphere from the stench of separation to the divine fragrance restoration. In front of people, you are always a couple. Some people want to see you arguing, struggling or even apart. That's why in front of people, you are always a couple. It's okay to disagree in the car or at home with each other. This doesn't mean that you're faking. It's considered being respectful of one another and showing the world that you stand together no matter what. No one will respect a man or a woman that will tear down their spouse in front of people.

Therefore, to enhance the resolution of infidelity between partners, share what it's like for each of you on both side of the experience. Try to obtain awareness and understanding of your individual behavior and emotional state through this process. If you are prepared to place as much drive into your marriage as you did into your affair, you will discover a new marriage. So, if the act of adultery has ever entered your thoughts, please remember, *"But a man who commits adultery has no sense: whoever does so destroys himself"* (Proverb 6:32/NIV).

CHAPTER ELEVEN

Accepting Trials

There is something within us that obviously attracts us and keeps us pressing toward new beginnings. The last couple of years (2019 – 2021, and counting) have been unprecedented and very difficult times for many who have lost loved ones due to the COVID-19 virus pandemic. The outlook of its end brings the hopefulness of a new beginning. However, let it be known that the anointing of the Holy Spirit is a vaccine to evil things and any virus that tries to come against us. We, as human beings, are obviously engineered for new beginnings. We are programmed to react to fresh incitements to measure our learning developments. This permits us to better understand life, ourselves and the normal order of things. It allows us to develop, thrust ahead into producing new levels, new discoveries, and acclimate. The continuous opportunity for new beginnings and the new discoveries they convey is a part of what makes us extraordinary.

To accomplish success, you need to begin from somewhere. Visions and aspirations come and go, and so do opportunities. However, if you're hoping to accomplish your vision, now is the best time to begin. If you're tired of starting over, then stop giving up!

Success is not looking for you while you're sitting back doing nothing to attain it. You must get moving, keep it moving, trust the process, and maintain a winning and victorious attitude. You can start your new beginnings from various life positions.

Unfortunately, most people can't figure out where to begin. This is primarily because their dreams are bigger, and they cannot find a way to initiate the process. Big dreams and visions always seem impossible until it's done. Remember, life is 10% what happens to you, and 90% how you respond. Trust God to lead, empower, energize, encourage, and bless you. If God has allowed you to see it, then it's been approved for you to be it. Go for it! Remember, prayer always comes before pursuit and execution. Go to God in prayer before you attempt to launch any vision, goal, or aspiration. This will enhance and confirm your confidence and provide you with the assurance that your steps are ordered. Once your confidence level has peaked, you can then press toward the high mark of the next level. Press toward those things that are essential as well as conceivable. This will provide and enhance your confidence level greatly. Gradually, you will begin accomplishing what seemed impossible at the beginning as well. Remember, always regulate your tolerance level, because when you pursue big visions, they may not come as fast as you want them to. For that reason, be patient, enjoy your journey, and trust the process!

God desires to see our progress. So much so, that He has given us reminders and assurances within His Word to ground and secure us in our faith. Psalm 92:12 reminds us, *"The righteous man will flourish like the palm tree; He will grow like a cedar in Lebanon."* This means that when we stay before God, He ensures that we, the righteous man, remain fresh, vibrant, and have the ability to grow in an enormous capacity. We will always be successful in producing fruit that is edifying to the Kingdom of Heaven. Cedars of Lebanon are amazingly large trees. They too, are always fresh and green. They are durable, and continually increase in virtue and happiness in the life of the truly righteous man, as opposed to the momentary, trifling, and perpetually decaying prosperity of the wicked.

How great and wonderful it is to experience the grace and blessings of God, which keeps us moving in spite of ourselves. As humans, we go through many difficult situations. Sometimes it seems as though our vision, goals and aspirations will never manifest themselves into what God has allowed us to see. Quite honestly, sometimes, our trials are challenging to experience. However, we were never meant to bear our trials. So, instead of asking God to remove our trials, we should be asking God for His strength and power so we can press and persevere through our difficulties. 2 Corinthians 12:7-8 says, *"Because of the extravagance of those revelations, and so I wouldn't get a big head, I was given the gift of a handicap to keep me in constant touch with my limitations. Satan's angel did his best to get me down; what he in fact did was push me to my knees. No danger then of walking around high and mighty! At first, I didn't think of it as a gift, and begged God to remove it. Three times I did that, and then he told me, My grace is enough; it's all you need. My strength comes into it's own in your weakness".*

This reminds us that there will surely be times when we don't understand or even agree with what God is doing in and through our lives. However, we as believers accept His will and our weaknesses. In all our new beginnings, we must see the value of our mistakes, failures, struggles and weaknesses and trust that God's grace is sufficient for us and that he lives within us always. So, whether our new beginnings start out good or not so good, we know that God is always there ensuring that things are working out for our good. Sometimes you must grow through what you go through. Your troubles and failures may not always be as severe as others.

On the other hand, what success looks like for one person may not look the same for another. However, Philippians 1:6 (NIV) reminds us that *"Being confident of this, that he who began a good work in you will carry it on to completion until the day of Christ Jesus."* There are always some kind of renovation going on in and around our lives. Usually, we focus on what the end results will be rather than focus on the complicated building process. It's during this time that we should examine ourselves and redefine success. Success is, *"the accomplishment of one's goal"* (Webster). So don't quit when things get hard.

Keep pressing, moving toward the promise, keep the faith, trust God's process, and keep obeying His Word.

It's only when we make God our highest priority, tenaciously seek and chase after Him, will we experience the best of life which is only attainable by the continuous pursuit of God. His benefits are eternal. Matthew 6:33 reminds us, *"But seek ye first the kingdom of God and His righteousness; and all these things shall be added unto you"*. God wants us to have good things such as, intimacy with him *(He's a loving and caring heavenly Father)*, satisfactions *(He wants our hearts to filled by Him)*, joy *(see our situations from a biblical standpoint)*, and his divine help *(we can go boldly to God in praye*r). Because of His grace and mercy, God is divinely changing our story! He's constantly pruning and purging us of the problems, circumstances, and people we have no need of; all of which has so easily beset us over the years.

The most important and destructive thing God purged from my life was unforgiveness. Unforgiveness is spiritually, mentally, and physically corrosive. It is impossible to initiate a new beginning successfully in the hells of unforgiveness. Unforgiveness is suppressed anger and resentment. The attributes of low self-esteem and the absence of self-love stem from not forgiving yourself or self-acceptance. Resentment and bitterness only enhance the possibility of depression and hopelessness. Before Nelson Mandela was released from prison, he stated, *"As I stand before the doorway of freedom, I realize that if I do not leave my pain, anger, and bitterness behind me, I will still be in prison".* Forgiveness does not make you weak, it sets you free. Setting out to pursue your vision and embarking on a new beginning requires all of you to be consumed by the Holy Spirit. If you are not totally surrendered, then you risk the potential of being infiltrated by negative attributes. Unforgiveness has the possibility of creating emotional storms of distress in which feelings of stress, anxiety, depression, resentment, lack of confidence, and fear all have a tendency of emerging. Unforgiveness also creates a hardened heart.

The hardened heart feels anger, resentment, bitterness, and hatred toward the offender. Unforgiveness is a sin that causes bitterness in our life. The Bible warns about bitterness: *"See to it that no one falls short of the grace of God and that no bitter root grows up to cause trouble and defile many"* (Hebrews 12:15, NIV). Just like a small root that grows into a tree, unforgiveness materializes in our hearts and dominates even our deepest Christian interactions and affairs. A "bitter root" comes when we accept frustration and disappointments and allow them to develop into resentment, or when we harbor our dislikes over previous pains. Resentment and unforgiveness do not just show up alone. They bring with them jealousy, animosity, discord, wickedness, and a host of other sinful attributes that you did not invite to the party! However, when the Holy Spirit consumes us, he can mend the pain that produces unforgiveness and bitterness.

You'll find that once you've allowed the Holy Spirit to soften and penetrate your heart, inject you with His love, joy, peace, forbearance, kindness, goodness, faithfulness, gentleness, and self-control (*as mentioned in Galatians 5:22*), He will then begin to stretch out in you, and you will begin to connect your life to His. John 15:4-5 says, *"Remain in me, as I remain in you. No branch can bear fruit by itself; it must remain in the vine. Neither can you bear fruit unless you remain in me. 'I am the vine; you are the branches. If you remain in me and I in you, you will bear much fruit, apart from me you can do nothing'"*.

Therefore, when we are connected and agree with the Holy Spirit, an even exchange of our illicit attributes for the qualities of His fruit occurs and begins to grow within us immediately. It will then resonate outside of us so that others may be able to witness and partake of the fruitful glory. *"O taste and see that the Lord is good: blessed is the man that trusteth in him"* (Psalm 34:8, NIV). We must take the first step in going after and obeying God. We'll realize that he's good, caring, compassionate toward us, and merciful. When we have faith in God, we will begin to encounter just how good God is. Then, and only then, are we adequately prepared and equipped to launch out and boldly pursuit our visions and new beginnings with confidence and blessed assurances, because our steps are ordered by God. Even though we know the Holy Spirit is guiding us, there is still so much left to know. Understanding God is like a continuous well. No matter how far you dig, you will never completely reach the bottom.

To pursuit God, is to get up every day ready and willing to dig deeper. It is to be overflowing to the top with God's love and spirit and yet desire more from Him. So, until God opens the next door of opportunity, start praising Him in the hallway! Some blessings tend to unfold while in the waiting process. However, believers do not have time to be stagnated and sitting around procrastinating about what we want to do and when we are going to do it. If God has given you a vision, He has equipped you to accomplish it! However, the timing belongs to God. Many times, in our excitement of what God has shown us, we get ahead of God and begin to implement strategies, ideas and even people, without prayer and consulting God. In our pursuit of God and the vision before us, we must never lose sight of God.

Remember, *"But seek first his kingdom and his righteousness, and all these things will be given to you as well"* (Matthew 6:33, NIV). Believers are to turn to God first so that all our visions, desires, thoughts, and ideas will take on the character of Christ. So be thankful and grateful for the successful outcomes that God has already promised and established for your new beginnings. God has special plans for you. However, He cannot establish you on the pathway to attaining His goals for your life until you identify your value and learn to love the person He has fashioned you to be.

CHAPTER TWELVE

Gratefulness

Psalm 100:4, NIV, tells us to *"Enter into his gates with thanksgiving and his courts with praise; give thanks to him and praise his name."* Therefore, remember God's kindness and trustworthiness, and then worship him with thanksgiving and praise. Psalm 118:1, NIV, also reminds us, *"Give thanks to the Lord, for he is good; his love endures forever."* I am a witness that every journey that I have been on has not always met with my expected outcomes. However, I am thankful that God brought me through every trial and difficult situation. Many of my best learning experiences have come through failures and setbacks. God has always been there to clean up my mess, lift, and bring me out of the muck and mire.

Therefore, I encourage you to remember that thanksgiving is a mindset of our heart. Having an attitude of gratitude indicates you do not just appreciate God for what He has done, but we appreciate Him for allowing new opportunities to be before us, for increasing and strengthening our faith, and for surrounding us with those that are like-minded. Thanking God beforehand is an affirmation of our love for Him and our faith in Him. God alone is more than worthy of our praise. When we come before God with a grateful heart, recognizing Him for who we are and all we have, then we are entering into his gates with thanksgiving.

When we bear witness to others with our testimonies of God's provisions and loving-kindness, then we are entering into his courts with praise. *"Behold, I will do a new thing; now it shall spring forth; shall ye not know it? I will even make a way in the wilderness, and rivers in the desert"* (Isaiah 43:19, KJV). Wow! God is telling us that he will even turn our meaningless, unfruitful wasteland into a lush place where others can benefit from the Living Water that flows from within you. Therefore, we do not have to be afraid of the past or the unknown, because God guides us, and places our feet upon the road to travel.

He even protects us along the way from all hurt, harm, or danger. However if you cannot distinguish the new thing God is doing or has done in your life from the past things, then you may want to check your vision. Sometimes we have a tendency to rely on our own peripheral vision instead of completely focusing on what God is doing or has done right in front of us. Close your eyes from the natural so that you can see better in the spirit! So, if you can't see it to change it, and you know God has allowed it, then find a way to prosper in it. Big things do not necessarily mean better. Small things can have a powerful impact on our lives if used correctly. *"For who hath despised the day of small things?...."* (Zechariah 4:10(a), KJV).

The question provides its own answer: none of us *should* despise the day of small things, because God has a perfect – though conceivably challenging – purpose for those days. God can do great things in small things! Satan is relying on you not realizing and believing that. Satan fears the day when you allow God to change the small things to great things in your life. Little things become much when placed into the Father's hands! Your vision and new beginnings may be small right now, but by the grace of God, He will educate, develop, and equip you for greater works if you will show yourself faithful over a few things. Small or big, God has fashioned us for His glory. Everything about us is important and a measure of His blueprint to inherit the lands. New beginnings can be fun, exciting, and pursued with the highest level of enthusiasm and tenacity. However, before we begin any journey, we must remember to die to ourselves. God and Satan have very different reasons for wanting us to die. Luke 9:23 says, *"And he said to them all, if any man will come after me, let him deny himself, and take up his cross daily, and follow me".*

Satan wants to destroy us by slander, while God wants to use those same lies to crucify our vulnerability to man's control. *"But God commandeth his love toward us, that, while we were yet sinners, Christ died for us"* (Romans 5:8, KJV). God knew a time would come when our lives would bless many people. Therefore, to inoculate us against the praise of man, He baptized us in the criticisms of man until we died to the opinions of man. You can't keep getting mad at people for sucking the life out of you if you keep giving them the straw. Even though we are accountable, we now live only for God's pleasure. Whether we please or offend man, that is God's business, not ours.

I am crucified with Christ, nevertheless I live; yet not I, but Christ liveth in me: and the life which I now live in the flesh I live by faith of the Son of God, who loved me, and gave himself for me" (Galatians 2:20, KJV). We die to self by being alive in Christ and less like ourselves. This means that we integrate Christ-like characteristics into our thinking and existence. Figuratively, this means more of God and less of us. To die with Christ is to allow our flesh to die, and make room for the Holy Spirit within us. Jesus Christ died for our sins on the cross. Consequently, dying to ourselves in this way is to cast our sins off, or let them die. Although we live our lives in the flesh, satisfying simple human needs, what is more important is satisfying the spirit. New beginnings can be long and tedious journeys. If you are anything like me, I do not like traveling alone.

I am what you might call "A People's Person." I love connecting and networking with others with a desire to effect positive change by establishing meaningful and edifying relationships. Over the years, I've learned that change will create you if you do not create change. Even if you resist or temporarily escape it, it will eventually find a way to enter your life. When you begin the change yourself, it's relatively easy to acclimate to it. I have been embracing change and new beginnings all throughout my adult life. Overall, when looking back over my life, I recognize that all the good things in my life are the outcomes of changes that happened in the past. Oftentimes, people ordinarily evade changes and choose to stay in their areas of comfort. I believe that once you find the courage to take the first step toward change, your life will come to be so much better, and will never be the same. I can understand why change can be difficult for some; fear of the unknown, unaware of your own inadequacies, fear of facing known inadequacies. However, change has its benefits. In a website blog written by Ani Alexander for Tinybuddha.com, she cited 10 powerful benefits of change and why we should embrace it.

They are as follows:

1. Personal growth

You grow and learn new things every time something changes. You discover new insights about different aspects of your life. You learn lessons even from changes that did not lead you to where you wanted to be.

2. Flexibility

Frequent changes make you easily adapt to new situations, new environments, and new people.

As a result, you do not freak out when something unexpectedly shifts.

3. Improvements

We all have things in our lives we would like to improve—finances, job, partner, house, etc. All of us know that nothing will improve by itself. We need to do things differently to make that happen. Without change, there would be no improvements.

4. Life values

From time to time changes make you re-evaluate your life and look at certain things from a different perspective. Depending on what the change is, it may also reinforce your life values.

5. The Snowball effect

Often, we give up because we cannot accomplish the difficult task of making a huge and immediate change. That is when small changes become extremely valuable. One shift at a time, small changes will eventually lead you to the desired big one.

6. Strength

Not all changes lead you to pleasant periods of life. Unfortunately, we do not live in fairy tale and sad things happen, too. Overcoming the tough period will make you stronger.

7. Progress

Changes trigger progress. Things move forward and develop because of the them.

8. Opportunities

One never knows what each change may bring. When you turn from your usual path there will be plenty of different opportunities waiting for you. Changes will bring new choices for happiness and fulfillment.

9. New beginnings

Each change is a turning page. It is about closing one chapter and opening another one. Changes bring new beginnings and excitement to life.

10. Routine

Remember the movie Stranger than Fiction? The main character Harold Crick does the same things in exactly the same time for years. He leads a completely dull, extremely predictable, and uninteresting life. That is how your life would be without changes.

So next time you get the temptation to avoid or resist the change, aim instead to initiate the ones that will lead you to where you want be.

And remember—if there were no change, there would be no butterflies.

New beginnings can be stimulating and encouraging and a very exhilarating time in your life. Everyone loves the idea of a fresh start and the outlook of accomplishing something different and exciting taking place in your life for a change.

It's great to feel stimulated because we all desire to live healthier lifestyles that permit us to give more and be more fruitful. Having a clean slate to work with can also help you learn from your previous blunders. A clean slate could be exactly what you need to get things turned around in your life. I've found that it helps to have a different and innovative openness to change. People can be set in their ways, thereby wrestling with change. Things may be going great in your life now, but as you begin to experience growth, you will realize that you're going in the wrong direction. Embracing your new beginnings allows you to be more open to change so that you don't end up remaining in the same place for long periods of time.

Having a fresh perspective of what you want, where you're going, and how to get there are critical to the vision. Perhaps your life simply thirsts for a fresh and creative perspective on things. Rather than seeing the adverse in everything, perhaps now you can see the positives. When you rise from your bed each day and see everything as a positive, you will be more likely to embrace change in your life and have a more optimistic viewpoint. This offers you balance in your life, which is what we all desire and require. If your life feels like it is going nowhere fast and you feel like you need a change, then you should explore a variety of training courses that can help develop you and bring your life in an entirely new direction. The only way that your life is going to change is if you make the changes yourself. *"The Lord our God said to us at Horeb, 'You have stayed long enough at this mountain'"* (Deuteronomy 1:6, NIV). So, get off your butt and get moving!

Change should come with expectations. Expectation means to imagine; to look forward to; to regard as likely to happen; to anticipate the occurrence or the coming of. Satan wants to reduce your vision, hinder your ability to move forward, obscure your vision, disrupt the start of your new beginnings, and erase your expected results. However, God is raising up somebody, somewhere, with power, finances, and resources, to provide for you and help you accomplish the vision. Help is on the way! New beginnings and visions couldn't be appreciated without opposition and moments of adversity that eventually season the journey with victory and accomplishment. New beginnings offer change. Change will test your faith and commitment to the vision. Change pushes you to that place of uncertainty. Change has a way of making you feel like you're in over your head. However, being in over your head is good because it demands that God be in it; that you don't rely on your own abilities.

All Christ-followers should consider themselves change agents for God. Change is the method by which the future occupies our lives. It causes us to escape out of the comfortable. I believe it is reasonable to assume that change is challenging for most people. Colossians 1:6 shows us how change in the people came when they received the Gospel and accepted it for themselves and began to bear fruits of faith. The Christian life is about spiritual growth and maturity. It is measureable, but at times slow, yet deliberate. You can see it mostly through our approach and choice changes in the life of one who diligently and tenaciously pursues and desires to follow Jesus Christ.

Our Faith in God makes change possible. Being content with where we are is a huge stepping-stone to moving toward your future. *"There are many of us that are willing to do great things for the Lord, but few of us are willing to do the little things"*.

- *Dwight L. Moody*

If you are faithful in the little things, you will be faithful in large ones. However, if you are dishonest and unfaithful in the little things, you won't be honest with the greater responsibilities. It sounds like an easy enough quest, because big changes and big projects may feel intimidating. However, the little things can be so hard to do. We often won't even consider the little things because they may seem silly, ridiculous, perhaps even useless. Our integrity often meets its match when it comes to matters of money. However, God calls us to be honest even in small details we could easily rationalize away. Don't let what you see and heard cause you to forget what God has promised you. The riches of heaven are far more valuable than earthly wealth.

Therefore, if we're not trustworthy with our money here (no matter how much or little we have), we will be unfit to handle the vast riches of God's kingdom. So don't allow your integrity to slip in small matters. It will not fail you in crucial and critical decisions either. *"Whoever can be trusted with very little can also be trusted with much, and whoever is dishonest with very little will also be dishonest with much. So if you have not been trustworthy in handling worldly wealth, who will trust you with true riches?"* (Luke 16:10 – 11, NIV). If you are faithful in the small things God is asking you to do, He will trust you with more.

CHAPTER THIRTEEN

The Blessing is Already Happening

Once you do the important things, that thing or situation where you might have had to humble yourself and serve somebody who doesn't treat you right, the door will open to the bigger things. Pass the small test! They're getting you prepared to handle the bigger and greater! Jesus humbled himself, came to earth, and became a servant that he might redeem us. Ask God to humble you like He did His Son, Jesus, and that you'll serve as Jesus did. God promised that if you are faithful in the small things, He will trust you with more.

Sometimes the most seemingly unimportant acts of faith (the little things, if you will) will work wonders. If only we would just get ourselves out of the way, open our minds to new opportunities and possibilities, and take a little step in faith. Remember, Solomon asked God for wisdom and God added wealth. Abraham asked God for a son, and God gave him generations. James 4:2 tells us, *"You desire but you don't have, so you kill. You covet (desire wrongfully) but you can't get what you want, so you quarrel and fight. You don't have because you don't ask God".* The biggest problem a believer experiences regarding prayer is not asking, but asking for the wrong things, and asking for the wrong reasons.

If you'll open your mouth and ask God for something greater than you and your right now, God promised that He'll open heaven and pour you out so many blessings that there won't be room enough for you to store it. Expect the great! Ask God for strength and strategy and watch your little become big. Expect means to imagine; to look forward to; to regard as likely to happen; to anticipate the occurrence or the coming of. However, when you're faithful, you'll experience some haters in your life. Haters are constantly attacking your vision; attacking your ministry. Satan wants to reduce your vision and work toward the greater things.

But, you see, God is raising up somebody, somewhere with their own money, resources, and abilities, to help you. What's coming is going to be better than what's been. Don't worry about how big your vision may seem, even if everyone is telling you *"you're in over your head."* Sometimes we need to be in over our heads because it demands that God be in it. However, the problem with some of us is that we've attached ourselves to something we were never assigned to, and now our vision is clouded and distorted. Haters are trying to get you to reduce the vision in half. However, God is sending you stronger leadership, better support, and committed investors to help you navigate the vision.

Don't worry about your haters, because there are more people with you than there are against you. God will allow people to gather around you to protect you right where you are. I pray that God will bless you with so much more than you ask for. Don't allow the world to squeeze you into a mold. It's easy to fit in and do what everybody else is doing, go where everybody else goes, think like everyone else thinks. Our friends complain and grumble, so we complain and grumble; our co-workers show up late, so we show up late; our loved ones struggle with addictions, so we struggle with addictions. It's common, but God didn't breathe His life into you so you would do what everybody else does.

You were created to be uncommon, live by a greater standard, do what others are not prepared to do, and have faith in things that others think are too big. God created us to stand out amongst the crowd and not settle for mediocrity. To be uncommon means, you're fervent about your future. You ask God for an increase, you're expecting the great, and you won't compromise your honesty. Romans 12:2 tells us, *"And be not conformed to this world: but be ye transformed by the renewing of you mind, that ye may prove what is that good, and acceptable, and perfect, will of God,"*

You do all you can to do the right thing when no one is looking, and you do your best to keep your word when it costs you something. Other people may not realize it, but we live by a higher standard. The reason is because we're uncommon. Paul urges Christians to respond to God's mercy, His forgiveness of our sin, and His inclusion of us in His family. The suitable response would be presenting our lives to Him as a living practice, a breathing sacrifice. Paul also tells us that we must no longer be conformed to the world. The word "world" is often used in the New Testament to refer to the "world system," or how every human being lives by default.

John described this worldly way of living as *"the desires of the flesh and the desires of the eyes and pride of life"* (1 John 2:16). Instinctively, we all pursue those things in search of pleasure and purpose. Paul tells us to abandon the pursuit of pleasure, possessions, and position—to stop living like everyone else. As an alternative, he strongly advises us to transform our minds. In detail, we must change how we think to have our minds renewed so that we can begin to comprehend and appreciate God's will for our lives.

God may continue to afford us the pleasure, possessions, and positions in various forms, but he encourages us to discover how to look at life with a new perspective: What is truly a good, acceptable, and perfect use of my life for His purposes and not just for my own? Some of the things you've been praying about and think will take years and years; God is going to deliver suddenly, unexpectedly, quicker than you thought. While you're praying for your healing, healing is already on the way. You're praying for your breakthrough, and the angel has already loosed the chains. So don't break before your breakthrough! God has already set your miracle into motion. God is still in the miracle-working business! You're going to hear a knock on your door sooner than expected. Psalms 56:9 says, *"the moment you prayed, the tide of the battle began to turn, and your miracle is about to come knocking at your door."*

John 1:1-3 says, *"In the beginning was the Word, the Word was with God and the Word was God, the same was in the beginning with God, all things were made by Him and without Him, was not anything made, that was made"*. Everything, and I mean *everythang*, including your vision and new beginnings, begins with the Word. You can shout, dance, run around the church, holler to the top of your lungs, speak in tongues, and jump all over the pews, but you haven't even got started until you get in the Word. I don't know what your situations or problems are, but I know that your answer, and your solution, is the Word of God.

Psalm 107:20 says, *He sent his Word and healed them and delivered them from all their destructions."* Your miracle is on the way! Faith is the hand that reaches out and takes hold of the blessings of God. However, the Word of God is what quickens the hand of faith. In Mark 3:5, Jesus commanded, *"Stretch forth thy hand"* to a man whose hand was withered, and at his Word, faith came alive."* It's not enough for The Word to pass by you every Sunday.

You have got to take hold of the Word and pull it into your world. Proverbs 4:20-22 says, *"My son, attend to my words; incline thine ear unto my sayings. Let them not depart from thine eyes; keep them in the midst of thine heart. For they are life, unto those that find them, and health, to all their flesh".* We serve a God who's able to supernaturally make things happen that we don't deserve. Thank God, that favor is chasing us down with unexpected blessings that all you can do is be amazed. So expect the great, and thank God that your miracle has been set in motion.

There is nothing that will impact our lives more than the power of prayer. Even in sports we "pray" for the home team to win. If they don't win, we are obviously disappointed, and we consider it an unanswered prayer. However, I believe that life's greatest tragedy is not unanswered prayer, but the failure *to* pray. Jesus is looking for kingdom disciples who will put his will over their own. Jesus is looking for followers, not fans. Instead of it being something we do every day, like breathing, eating, and walking and talking, it seems to have become like that little glass covered box on the wall that says, "Break in case of emergency." It's true that so very often we associate prayer with crises in our life.

I remember reading about a story of a man who encountered a bit of trouble while flying his little airplane. He called the control tower and said, *"Pilot to tower, I'm 300 miles from the airport, six hundred feet above the ground, and I'm out of fuel. I am descending rapidly. Please advise. Over." "Tower to pilot,"* the dispatcher began, *"Repeat after me: "Our Father Who art in heaven...".* Prayer is, for the most part, an untapped and invaluable resource, and unexplored place where indescribable treasure remains to be uncovered. It's discussed more than anything else, but regrettably, practiced less than anything else. Yet, for the believer, it continues to be one of the greatest gifts God has provided for us separate of salvation.

Paul was somebody who thoroughly understood prayer and its power. Prayer was an important part of Paul's life. However, he took it for granted that it would be a part of the life of every Christian. You can't really be a good Christian and not pray, just like you can't have a good marriage if you don't talk to your spouse. You can't be messy and anointed. Having a bad and messy attitude can literally block you from love, blessings, and destiny from finding you. Don't be the reason you don't succeed. Prayer is the conduit of communication between God and His people, between God and those who love Him. Believers must pray with persistence (tenacity), especially while discouraged. Paul reminds us in Colossians 4:2 by saying, *"Devote yourselves to prayer, being watchful and thankful"* (NIV). Our persistence is an expression of our faith that God answers our prayers. Our prayers and faith shouldn't dictate how fast or slow God is moving. Delays or repeating issues may be God's way of working and maneuvering His will in our lives. In other words, we are to "*Continue earnestly in prayer,*" Colossians 4:2(a), NKJV.

CHAPTER FOURTEEN

Devotion Of Prayer

"Devote yourselves" carries with it the idea of dedication.

Of the ten times it is used in the New Testament four of them have to do with being devoted to prayer. It's a very powerful word and in this verse is given as an imperative, or a command. In other words, persistence in prayer is not an option for the Christian it is an order from the Lord Himself. Two of the most instructive parables Jesus ever told on prayer, one in Luke 11 and the other in Luke 18, both have to do with being persistent and not giving up in prayer. Luke 11: 9 & 10 is where we find the promise that says, *"ask and it shall be given to you; seek and you shall find; knock and it shall be opened to you."* This teaches us that we shouldn't grow weary in our prayer life.

Keep on asking, keep on seeking, keep on knocking, keep on believing, keep on praying, keep on praising, keep on worshiping, keep on moving, keep on preaching, keep on teaching, keep on until you get your breakthrough! Jesus doesn't want us to give up in prayer, He instructs us to be persistent. Luke 18:1 says, (The Persistent Widow) *"Jesus told His disciples a parable to show them that they should always pray and not give up."*

Always means "keep on!" God has a reason why He's delaying and allowing. God wants our faith and hope to grow, not cease! So, don't give up! Now there is a difference between a persistent prayer and a long prayer. A persistent person in prayer doesn't necessarily have to pray for a long time.

God doesn't need your painfully long, vain repetitious, 3-hour prayers. Persistence means not giving up. Some people give up easy. They quit because they say they don't feel like praying. The joy is gone. The feeling is gone. Nevertheless, we are not to live by our feelings but to live by the commandments of our Lord who tells us to pray without ceasing. And every time we see Jesus praying, He was praying with passion. In Luke 3:1 at His Baptism - while He was praying, the heaven was opened. Passionate prayer opens Heaven. In Luke 6:12, before He called His disciples - He spent the whole night in prayer. Passionate prayer gives direction. In Luke 9:29 at His transfiguration, and _while_ He was praying, the appearance of His face became different, and His clothing became white and gleaming. Passionate prayer enables us to experience the glory of the Father. Jesus always prayed with passion, because He knew Who He was talking to. He knew that prayer to the Father is powerful and not something to take lightly and casually. The successful outcomes of our new beginnings rely primarily on a healthy prayer life and the right relationship with God the Father.

For our new beginnings, there are new endings. New beginnings can provide a certain level of excitement. However, some endings can be catastrophic and tragic. It could be a close or marital relationship, a ruined vision, a business venture that didn't survive, or a loved one who passed away. This can be difficult for us because an ending can feel like a hindrance, and oftentimes it feels like a disaster. Nevertheless, just as God opens a door for a new beginning, He also closes doors and ends things. The reason He closes a door is not that he intends to deprive us of any good thing, but that He has something greater in store for us.

As an alternative to being bitter, losing your joy, and being down and out, I suggest rejoicing through your issues, knowing that your breakthrough is on the way. So go ahead and say farewell to the pain, the problems, the frustrations, and the depression. Quit beating yourself up. Stop carrying letdowns from yesterday into today. Receive it as part of God's design, be at peace with what's behind you, and move forward. When you say goodbye to your past, it releases you into the freedom of your future. So glorify God the Father and bless Him that he has been your Alpha and Omega, your beginning and end. We can be free and confident in trusting God with our achievements and accomplishments, and we can trust Him with what ends and what doesn't make sense to us.

Trust and believe that God is in complete control and is guiding our future. *"I am the Alpha and Omega, the beginning and the ending, saith the Lord, which is and which was, and which is to come, the Almighty"* (Revelations 1:8, KJV). We get excited about new beginnings. We talk a lot about God being the Alpha and doing new things, but we don't hear much about how He, the Omega, brings things to an end. It could be a relationship, a broken dream, a business that didn't make it, or a loved one who passed away. This is hard for us because an ending can feel like a setback, and often it feels like a failure. But just as God opens a door, He closes doors and brings things to an end. The reason He closes a door is because He has something better. Instead of being sour and losing your joy, the best thing you can do is to just say goodbye to the hurt, the questions, the disappointment, and the self-pity. Quit beating yourself up; quit bringing failures from yesterday into today.

Accept it as part of God's plan, be at peace with what's behind you, and move on. When you kiss the past goodbye, it releases you into your future. In an article written by Heidi Richards-Mooney for Thrive Global website entitled, *"Say Hello to New Beginnings and Goodbye to Things that Must End: The Art of Starting Fresh (2018),"* Richards-Mooney stated, *"An ending can only come when you let go of thinking about them. When negative things get to be beyond your control, you've got to distance yourself and begin to make a space for the positive. Otherwise, it will interfere with the future you want to have and keep you from making the changes you need to make.*

Get a grip on the reality of endings. You don't have to like all of them, but you do need to accept the reality of what they are. If you don't learn to accept endings to allow for new beginnings, you could simply give up and that would mean unhappiness and a lifetime of regrets. Think about things in a new way. You may think of yourself as "set in your ways," about certain things, but you have the right to change your mind if something occurs (such as more knowledge) to tilt your thinking another way. Sometimes it helps to gain a fresh perspective on life and let go of old beliefs".

Although you may not agree with everything Richards-Mooney conveys in her article. One thing is true and sure is that negative and positive cannot occupy the same space. Sooner or later, you're going to have to decide on how you want your journey to end. Sometimes you must simply make a move and realize that there's so much more to you than where you are. Don't be afraid to step out on faith! Some chapters of your life filled with hurt, pain, and despair need to be closed and never read again. There comes a time when you have to develop your life and reap the benefits and rewards. You deserve it! Stop trying to fix your broken past, and let God create a greater future for you. Don't worry about your haters and nay-sayers. Somebody is always out there discussing the "old you" because they don't have access to the "new you." Don't forget that in Luke 23:28, they thought when they crucified Jesus and hung the sign above him while he was on the cross, *"THIS IS THE KING OF THE JEWS"* that it was the end of him. But what Satan didn't realize was that because of Jesus' physical death, he was just coming into his spiritual kingdom, His new beginning.

Just like Jesus, there are some things you're going to have to kill off and let the world have while you casually and spiritually step off into your new beginnings. And just like Jesus is King of the Jews (and the whole universe), you too, can embrace your new beginnings with boldness and confidence. Satan was hoping you would crumble from your past and the death of your flesh, but Jesus struck a death blow to Satan's rule. We win, and now reign with Jesus Christ through His eternal authority over our new beginnings.

Since God the Father is the eternal Lord and Ruler of the past, present, and future, we know that without God, we have nothing eternal. Nothing can change our lives for the good and save us from sin. Therefore, always worship, praise, and honor the One who is the beginning and the end of all existence, wisdom, and power. This will help you remain focused on the new positives and let your haters bask in the old negatives.

Whether good or bad, all beginnings must and will end. The Roman philosopher, Seneca, once stated, *"Every new beginning comes from some other beginning's end."* As you venture on the way to your next objectives and new beginning, the excitement of creativity and innovation should be highly anticipated. However, at the same time, you may be subjected to a sense of misfortune for what had moved out before, particularly if things didn't happen the way you intended. Unfortunately, this can occur with spiritually blurred vision, unexpected developments, and questionable relationships.

For every new beginning, there must be a vision. Vision is a vital component of your new beginnings and successful endings. Remember that God is the Alpha and Omega, the beginning and the end, and He loves us so much that He sees us through all of our life journeys. Without Him, all of our selfish beginnings would meet with temporal and unproductive results. It is a blessing to know that whatever we face, Jesus is always there to protect and provide us with his inclusive love and encouraging power. Therefore, Jesus must be the primary and integral part of our beginnings and endings, the author and finisher of our faith.

I've found that if you want to experience a productive life, one that is pleasing to God, it helps to pay more attention to the beginnings than the endings. So many people say they want to experience the blessings of a new life; however, they take the new one God has set before them for granted. Don't allow this to happen to you. You can't embrace what's no longer there. Don't wait until your life is nearly over to recognize how invaluable and irreplaceable the current moment is. So, appreciate and take advantage of your here and now!

Step out on faith! The good life is before you, and it starts right now! So, be humble. Remain teachable. The world is so much greater than your vision of the world. So, enjoy your new beginnings! There's always space for a fresh start, a new step… a new beginning. Embrace it. God bless you!

References

https://thriveglobal.com/stories/new-beginnings-and-final-endings/

10 Powerful Benefits of Change & Why We Should Embrace It (tinybuddha.com)

Jentezen Franklin entitled, *"The Five Ingredients of an Anointing"*

www.ingramcontent.com/pod-product-compliance
Lightning Source LLC
Chambersburg PA
CBHW021653120626
46545CB00002B/834